# Threads
## of
# Gold

*by*

# Elaine Perry

Published by:

McDougal Publishing
P.O. Box 3595
Hagerstown, MD 21742-3595
www.mcdougalpublishing.com

McDougal Publishing is a ministry of The McDougal Foundation, Inc., a Maryland nonprofit corporation dedicated to spreading the Gospel of the Lord Jesus Christ to as many people as possible in the shortest time possible.

ISBN: 978-1-58158-185-0

Printed in the United States of America
For Worldwide Distribution

# Dedication

*To Father God:* Thank You for choosing me to be part of the Bridal Company. (It was His idea to write the book, not mine.)

*To Yeshua, Jesus, our Bridegroom-King:* Thank You that I am accepted in the Beloved, and You have gone to prepare a place for me to be with You, eternally Yours. (The book is all about Him and getting to know Him intimately.)

*To the Holy Spirit, who is my best friend and who has been preparing me and will present me on my glorious wedding day:* You have led me all the way through to the end.

# Acknowledgements

We are surrounded by a great cloud of witnesses, both seen and unseen, and there have been people with me in this particular race from the beginning, from the moment of hearing the starting gun until now, to help me avoid false starts and let the timing of the release of this book be perfect. These include my husband Roy, family members, friends, intercessors who have cheered me on in every lap of the race and some who have been added later, even grandchildren who were not even born in the beginning, but who are now cheering me on to the finish line.

Two particular women have been added to this last lap. The first is Margriet Hintz, who has blessed me financially and become the producer, as well as an intercessor, for me to complete the race. She is an exhorter and has been faithful and has been a joy to me since being given to me as a gift from Papa God.

The second is Gloria Reid, who asked me to write a short teaching for her oils and then released me to drop that idea and just write what was in my heart to write. She gave me her permission to include her anointing oils here, and this brought depth and understanding. I want to honor both of these women, apart from my other friends who have interceded for me and never gave up.

I thank my husband for his unselfish confidence in my gifting and determination to do whatever the Holy Spirit asks me to do for the King and his technical assistance when I couldn't see how to get my handwritten notes into typed form. Roy, we wrote this book together. As has been the norm throughout our years of marriage, you have been the quiet strength as my unseen hero. You always allow me solitude to pursue our beloved God. Thank you for making room in the inn of your heart and our home so that I may be Holy Spirit inspired to write. As I write these words, today it is Veteran's Day here in the United States. Names of fallen heroes are being read aloud all day long, to acknowledge their lives. You, my beloved husband, are remembered in my book of honor for all to know that I respect and love you. Thank you for demonstrating the Bridegroom's fragrant heart to me.

I am indebted to Harold McDougal, my editor. I was able to give my baby (book) over to you without fear of it being dissected and becoming unrecognizable. Your patience and the trust I have for you are truly gifts from our heavenly Father. Thank you is not enough to say for how much I owe to your contribution.

To all of those close to me: I am so humbled by your love and faithfulness. You are listed on my Hall of Fame and Honor. Hear your names called. Since this has been a marathon and not a sprint, there are many. Since I didn't have my natural parents to help me, my heavenly Father sent me a large group of siblings to inspire and encourage me. At the risk of leaving some names out I will try and group them together:

My coaches in Christ: Nancy Herbert, Margriet Hintz, Mary Ellen Wright, Alison Kern, Amanda Perry, Linda Vaughan, Gloria Reid, Linda Kahler, JoJo, Dorcas, all my Pennsylvania sisters, Marilyn Weigands, and all my Canadian brothers and sisters.

My spiritual advisors, Bob and Shelley, thank you for "parenting" me through prayer ministry and friendship beyond.

Thank you, Canadians intercessors, for your prayers and acceptance of me, feeding me great food and teaching me your culture and language, *eh?!*

Lastly, thank you for the numerous brothers (and spiritual sons) who gave me great insight and interceded for me. A few are: Bob Griffin, Neil, Wade, Jesse, Tom, Fred, Bill Yount, Peter McCall, Nathan Kern, Adam Perry, Matthew, and so many more seen by our Father and rewarded by Him alone. *Merci!*

# Contents

**Revelation 22:17**

*The Spirit and the bride say,*
*"Come!"*
*And let him who hears say,*
*"Come!""*
*Whoever is thirsty let him*
*come;*
*and whoever wishes, let him*
*take the free gift of the water of*
*life.*

# *Introduction*

**Habakkuk 2:2-3 (One New Man)**

*The Lord answered me and said:*

*"Write the vision and make it plain on tablets,*
*That he may run who reads it,*
*For the vision is yet for an appointed time,*
*but at the end it will speak and it will not lie,*
*Though it tarries, wait for it; it will surely come.*
*It will not tarry."*

NEITHER THE IDEA TO write this book nor its title were my own. Rather, I was commissioned by the Father to write it, and He named it what pleased Him. The message of the book was conceived on my knees in the 1980s, as I was deeply immersed in prayer and worship. I was in my bedroom when, all of a sudden, my spiritual eyes were opened by the Holy Spirit. I saw a vision, or picture, of an extremely bright light surrounding a book. I was drawn to see this mystery, as Moses was to keep looking at the burning bush.

As I drew closer to the book, a glory was emanating around it, within it, and from it. In other words, the book was saturated in what the Holy Spirit called "prophetic glory." I said to the Lord, "This must be Your Holy Word," meaning the Scriptures.

He replied, "No, Elaine, this is the book you will write for Me, and it will be perfectly illustrated."

He continued, "The name of the book is *Threads of Gold.*"

I hid that word in my heart and waited to see what else the Holy Spirit would reveal to me.

But what would be the topic of the book? I had a title but no idea of what I was to write in the book. It was to be a long time before I finally knew.

The Scriptures have said:

**Deuteronomy 19:15**

*A matter must be established by the testimony of two or three witnesses.*

As time went by, I began to doubt if I was ever going to write the book and even wondered at times if I had actually seen the vision. I cried out to the Lord, and He sent me encouragement through various witnesses.

My first and continual encouragement was from my husband Roy. When I shared with him about writing a book for the Father, his faith was high. He told me I *would* write the book and fulfill my destiny, just as Abba had told me. And Roy's faith was unwavering throughout the years to come.

My second witness came through a prophetic dream encounter. I was living in Kansas City, Missouri, at the time, had been immersed in the prophetic for quite a while, and was in relationship with many prophets and prophetic intercessors. During this particular encounter, a large angel came to me, along with a prophet I knew named Bob Jones. The three of us went together up into the heavens and came to stand before a huge door. I realized that it was a heavenly library and immediately sensed that this was just one of many.

The angel opened the door to us, and we were led inside. There we saw shelf upon shelf lined with volumes of books. I was in awe!

The angel then led me to a certain section of the library. I looked up to read a sign saying, "Autobiographies." I cannot describe the weightiness of fiery glory that was upon those books.

The angel took down one of the books and placed it inside me, and as it unfolded within my spirit, I felt a fire released. It was the first time I had any idea about what was to be in the book I was commissioned to write. I had been seeking for this answer for years.

My third witness came to confirm the title of the book. At the church our family was attending, in Blue Springs, Missouri, was an older man (in his eighties) who was a well-known prophet to the city. His name was Joseph. He was now becoming quite weak due to illness, and it was evident that he would soon go home to be with the Lord. Joseph and I had a relationship, and he called one morning to ask me if I was going to the church that day for intercessory prayer. I was surprised by this and answered, "Yes, why?"

He told me he'd had a dream and was coming to the church to prophesy over me and wanted to do it in the presence of the pastor.

When we met at the church, our pastor and everyone else who was there was shocked that Joseph had come, since he was in such a weakened state.

Joseph began by asking me if the Lord had told me to write a book. I was very surprised, for I had told no one about it except my husband and family. I said, "Yes."

He said that he'd had a dream in which he saw a book, and glory was coming from it. He went closer to examine the book, and when he saw my name on the cover, said, "Oh, I know that author."

Next he said, "I even know the title of the book: *Threads of Gold!*"

Well, this about did me in, because I had never told a soul as yet about the title — not even my family.

One more confirmation came when Joseph said, "Oh yes, and it will be perfectly illustrated." Praise God! It was many years later before I received more understanding about what *Ruach HaKodesh* meant by this statement.

At first I thought I would have to find a person who was a great illustrator and could draw perfect pictures for the book. But as time went on, and I began to preach this revelation of the Bride, a friend of mine came up to me after the service one day. She happened to be an artist, and she said to me, "Elaine, you think you have no artistic talent, but every time you get up and preach on this encounter, you illustrate it perfectly with your words." She told me to look up Psalm 45:1. I did that. It said:

**Psalm 45:1 (AMP)**
*My heart overflows with a goodly theme; I address my psalm to a King. My tongue is like the pen of a ready writer.*

The Holy Spirit is the perfect Illustrator, and He was to give me the word illustrations for the book.

**Revelation 1:36 (KJV)**
*Keep those things which are written ... , for the time is at hand.*

When the fourth and final witness was given to me, it was regarding the timing, the when of being released to actually write the book. The Holy Spirit told me I would not release the book until my mother had passed on to be with the Lord.

## Threads of Gold

While I was on a mission trip to South Africa, I met a prophet named Neil Kleinhaus. Just after our initial meeting, Neil asked me if I had been commissioned to write a book. I told him I had and asked why? He said the Holy Spirit wanted me to rest in the timing and not to be concerned until after my mother had gone home. Mom went home to be with Jesus in 2008, so I knew the time was nearing.

When I met Neil, I had been studying the Song of Songs for six years. He confirmed that this was to be the thread of the book. He also said it would have a breaker anointing upon it.

Along with all of these prophetic reminders, numerous scriptures were quickened to me relating to holding on to God's promises. This proved to be so necessary because the entire process has been drawn out over more than twenty-five years. I am so thankful that the Lord kept reminding me throughout that long wait. It did tarry, but now it has come.

As amazing as it might seem, it is only now, as the book goes to press, that I fully understand the meaning of its title. My story could not be told in the normal way, chronologically. It had to be told in threads, as the Spirit revealed them. Here, then, is *Threads of Gold*.

*Elaine Perry*
*Ogdensburg, New York*

## The Emerging Bride

Come down, Lord Jesus, in all Your

glory,

With all Your authority,

With all Your multi-faceted anointing.

Come down,

Right into our midst,

Right into our circumstance,

Stun us with Your awesome presence.

Silence us with Your all-consuming fire.

Renew us with Your ever-washing Word.

Capture us with Your ever-loving

eyes of compassion.

Part I

# Bridal Preparation

Chapter 1

# Come Away, My Beloved

**Revelation 22:17**
> *The Spirit and the bride say "Come!"*

**Song of Songs 2:10 (AMP)**
> *Rise up, my love, my fair one, and come away.*

MY BELOVED SPOKE THIS to me, and my preparation for being part of the emerging Bride started many years ago. The entire story would be very long, but I must at least tell you how the Holy Spirit called me and then chose me. Jesus said:

**Matthew 22:14 (AMP)**
> *For many are called (invited and summoned), but few are chosen.*

He spoke these words at the end of what we have come to call the Parable of the Wedding Feast. Every believer is called to be part of this feast, but not all will choose to go through the necessary preparations, only those who have dove's eyes, those who see only Him and love only Him.

I was called by the Holy Spirit through words like *emerging* and *longing*. I would hear Him speaking these words to me, and then I would pursue on to know what He was saying about them.

About two weeks before I heard the actual term *the emerging Bride,* I had received a prophetic word from the Lord in which He told me that I was now getting ready to emerge from the season I had been in. This word *emerge* was quickened to me like a child leaping in my womb, and I bore witness with it. Then, like Mary, I hid that word in my heart ... until a couple of weeks later I was online one day.

At this point, I must confess that I am technically-challenged. I can get online and find wonderful sites, but I then have no idea how I got there or how to get back there even if I want to. So what I do find is truly Holy Spirit led and inspired.

On this particular day I was online to see what I could discover about anointing oils. I am a *fragranceholic,* if there is such a term (and if there isn't, there should be). I love the fragrances of the Lord, so I wanted to see what other people were saying about them. I stumbled onto a site that listed fragrant anointing oils, and I began to read the names of each oil.

The power of the Holy Spirit came upon me (as it is even now as I am writing these words), and it increased as I continued to read about these special oils. I could feel the weightiness of His presence in them. I thought, "My word, if just the names of these oils are so anointed, I would like to know more about them." I eagerly scrolled down to read more, but there was no more information, just a phone number to call. I later learned that the woman who had listed the oils hadn't yet created her website and was just using a friend's site to introduce her oils to the public. It was a divine setup.

I proceeded to call the number indicated, and a lady answered. I told her I was interested in her anointing oils and would like more information about them. She was kind, but told me she was at lunch with some other people, and she took my number and promised to call me back that night after work. I did learn that her name was Gloria, but not much more. So she was Gloria (glory), and I was Elaine (light). "Not a bad combination!" I thought.

Later that evening Gloria Reid and I did connect by phone, and there was an immediate bonding. She explained to me that she was an apothecary for the Lord and had just finished pouring a new set of oils she had named Emerging Bride. That brought tears to my eyes, for this was my language. I loved anything that had to do with the Bride.

I was a little saddened to learn that this particular set of oils had been set apart, to be poured out before the Lord first in Jerusalem, and that this would not take place until a few months later.

As we continued to share what was in our hearts, the Holy Spirit knitted us together, and I dared to ask if she would pray about sending me some of the oil. Before hanging up that evening, we exchanged addresses, and she felt released to mail me samples of her special oils. A beautiful friendship had begun.

Now I need to backtrack to give you a better idea of how all of this fit into my life:

In 1984 I was going through an extremely difficult time. I had just learned that I had breast cancer and would need a double mastectomy. I was pressing into the Lord daily for eight hours or more, not so much seeking my healing or a miracle (which, of course, I wanted), but I sensed that what I needed was more of Jesus.

One day, during this time, while I was in deep worship, my room began to fill with the glory of the Lord. I felt impressed to get up off the floor where I had been praying and stand. I heard music in my spirit, and I began to dance to the sound of it. In that moment, the tangible presence of God's glory was on me, as if a garment had fallen over me, and I heard the Lord say to me, "May I have this dance?"

In my spirit, I saw Jesus standing there. His arms were opened to me, and He was ready to dance. As I approached Him, instead of us dancing as partners do, facing each other, me following His lead, we blended together into one and danced in that way. As I danced with the Lord, I was in Him, and He was in me. It was a perfect unity, a perfect oneness.

In the gospel that bears his name, John recorded these words from Jesus' prayer to the Father:

**John 17:22-23 (AMP)**

> *I have given to them the glory and honor which You have given Me, that they may be one [even] as We are one: I in them and You in Me, in order that they may become one and perfectly united, that the world may know and recognize that You sent Me and that You have loved them [even] as You have loved Me.*

When I finished dancing with Jesus, I was given a prophecy (which I have included in the explanation associated with the oil, Two Camps of Oil). The entire time we danced I could smell a holy and intimate fragrance. It was so divine, never to be forgotten.

I also saw white roses, and the petals of those roses were scattered much like a flower girl spreads petals down the aisle in a wedding, preparing the way for the coming bride.

Without a doubt, our Lord was preparing me for something special.

Chapter 2

# Just Say Yes

FROM THAT TIME ON, I was led to meet daily with the Holy Spirit, and He opened up to me the song we had danced to. It was the Song of Dance, the Song of Songs, the Song of the King. He taught me from His Word about becoming the Bride, and I said yes to His invitation.

What I call "His invitation" is, in reality, a command from the King, and yet, we, as His Bride, have the choice to answer or not. We can say yes, or we can say no. The Bride must consent always, for He will never force us into betrothal out of duty or obligation. Ours can only be a union of love.

Saying yes to our Bridegroom is all it takes to begin the preparation, and we continue the preparation in the same way, always saying yes to His subsequent proposals. It is yes to the Bridegroom's heart and then yes to the costly preparation the Holy Spirit wishes to accomplish in us. It is the Spirit and the Bride that say, *"Come,"* but she must wait upon the Holy Spirit to prepare her for her loving King *Yeshua*.

Like Queen Esther, we must agree to the six months of oils and six months of spices. We must say yes and yes and yes again — all along the way. I was learning what was expected of a king's bride, and with each step, I was saying a resounding YES!

Chapter 3

# The Pageant

BEFORE MY SURGERY I had one more encounter with the Lord. It was during Passover, at the end of March or early April, while our family was attending a city-wide Easter pageant. It was an amazing site, with real live animals (even camels) and a full-blown theatrical presentation. This was before they began charging for the event, so there was standing room only, and we had to be seated along one side wall in folding chairs.

As the pageant began, I found myself enthralled with its beauty. The story of the resurrection had always been a cornerstone of my faith in Jesus. Now, as I sat there, a cloud of God's glory again came over me. It enveloped me, and I heard clearly, "See how they celebrate Me — My birth and My death and resurrection?"

I said, "Yes, Lord, I do see."

Then He said, "But they do not know that this is not the face I will present to them when I return. They do not recognize *that* face."

"What is that face, Lord?" I asked.

He said, "The face of the Bridegroom-King!"

Just then, as He spoke, I was shown in the Spirit, like a play would be viewed in different acts, five distinct acts.

In Act I, I was the Bride. She was dancing, and she received colors from the five-fold ministries to wear different shades of scarves of a silky flowery material. She would take one and put it around her waist and freely dance on until she got the next color. By the end of the first act, she was wearing all of the covenant colors.

He then showed me Act II. The Bride was at the feet of Jesus, worshiping Him. She declared who He was, she wept, and her tears would wash His feet. She continued to worship Him and declare His worth to her.

Next, He stooped down and picked His Bride up, and looking deep into her eyes (both of them now eye-to-eye), began to declare and prophesy over her all that she was to Him and all that she was to be. He said He had given her His name, His nature, His character, His power, His glory, and His love. It all belonged to her now. How glorious!

As the psalmist declared:

**Psalm 45:11 (One New Man)**

> *Then the King will desire your beauty, because He is your Lord (Adonai), bow down to Him.*

As Act II ended, the Bride was bowing at His feet in adoration and separation.

Act III was pure worship and adoration, with great joy, angels coming to celebrate and also to help prepare the Bride for the wedding feast.

Act IV was solemn consecration, the Bride getting full of peace and grace and coming to understand her covenant relationship with her Beloved.

Act V was the ceremony of betrothal under the *chuppah,* or bridal canopy. It was all breathtakingly beautiful!

Chapter 4

# I Saw His Face

AS I GAZED AT THE *chuppah*, all I could see was light, golden light, like a brilliant canopy formed over the Bride, and I saw for the first time that face, the face with which He will return at the end of the age, the face of the Bridegroom-King.

Only two words came to me as I gazed on that brilliant and glorious face: "Holy desire." He was all I would ever desire again. He is what could only satisfy me. He was not only my entire personal desire, but also the desire of all the nations.

To me, He was irresistible. He was my Beloved, He was my Bridegroom, He was the Lover of my soul, He was my All in All, He was my Lord and King!

*Ruach Hadesh*, the Holy Spirit, has quickened me to give clarity to this word *desire*. It is a holy desire, meaning "having pleasure in." To say it clearly, David said, in Psalm 63:1:

> *My body [kamah] yearns [or desires] for you, in a dry and weary land where there is no water.*

## Threads of Gold

The Hebrew word translated here as *longs* or *desires* is *comah* or *kamah* meaning "desired, yearned for, or longed for." As I saw the Lord as holy desire, there was imparted, through His eye gates into mine, insight and perception pertaining to having a single eye and being full of light. Seeing Him birthed a desire in me to be the closest I could be to His heart and to tabernacle, or dwell, there with and in Him. It also birthed in me, the Bride, the desire to be constantly in Him, fellowshipping and following Him wherever He might lead.

I desired to be fully and wholly identified with Him. I would take His name and all that this invoked. The Lamb's wife follows Him wherever He leads her, and I will follow Him too.

Yes, He is the desire of all nations, as Psalm 73:25 states, and upon seeing His face, or countenance, I then longed to have a more personal, fuller experience with my Messiah.

Seeing Him — Holy Desire, Bridegroom-King — stirred within me bridal affection for the Adonai of Glory. His eyes full of holy desire for me communicated His deep affection as the Lover of my soul. May His face, countenance, shine upon us and give us grace.

I once again heard His voice, and He said to me, "Go and tell them how I am returning as the Bridegroom. They have not prepared to be one with Me. As they hunger and thirst for Me, I will give them bridal affection."

I said, "Yes, Lord, I will tell them, but more importantly, I want to be part of the bridal company, Your Bride."

I was now back in my awareness of the resurrection pageant, which was ending, and everyone was asking me how I had enjoyed it. I had to tell them that I hadn't seen any of it because I had been caught up into God's fiery presence.

Moses wrote:

**Deuteronomy 29:29**

> *The secret things belong to the Lord our God [Adonai our Elohim], but the things revealed belong to us and to our children forever.*

In his second letter to the Corinthians, Paul explained what happens when we "see":

**2 Corinthians 3:18 (AMP)**

> *And all of us, as with unveiled face, [because we] continued to behold [in the Word of God] as in a mirror the glory of the Lord [Elohim], are constantly being transfigured into His very own image [the Bridegroom] in ever increasing splendor and from one degree of glory to another; [for this comes] from the Lord [Who is] the Spirit.*

I had to tell that much of my testimony so that you could realize how immersed I became in the Bride and Bridegroom paradigm. It was all-consuming and would continue to be.

Chapter 5

# *The Anointed Oils*

FOR THE NEXT FIFTEEN years, every year on my birthday my Bridegroom, *Yeshua*, would give me a new fragrance to wear. These were perfumes I could purchase from the world, but each one had a prophetic meaning for me. As I was waiting to hear from Him which fragrance to wear for the sixteenth year, He spoke to me to wear Eternity Moments, but He also said, "This is the last earthly perfume. You will wear no more perfume made from the world's scents."

He then led me to a company in Israel that had anointing oils poured for specific purposes and prepared by anointed hands for biblical principals. These anointing oils would now be what He would give me to wear (and to walk out their prophetic meanings). I would personally apply them to my own walk, as I prepared to be the Bride, and as I made intercession for others to come into the Bride relationship. Thus, I began a journey of wearing Abba Oils for years. This is how I was to be trained and fine-tuned, like Esther, to the fragrances of the Lord for His Beloved.

In 2010, when I came across the new anointing oils being poured by Gloria Reid, I had accumulated, like Mary of Bethany, all of His oils inside my alabaster jar (my heart). It just so happens that I was born at Bethany Hospital (in Kansas City, Kansas) and have identified with the heart of Mary of Bethany my entire life.

For seven years I spent time alone in my room with my dear friend, the Holy Spirit, as He taught me from the Word, not only from the Songs of Songs, but from other brides, such as Eve, Ruth, Deborah, Esther, the Marys, and even David and John the Beloved. I was to walk out the Song of Songs with my own natural and beloved husband Roy before I would be allowed to go and teach, or demonstrate, the face of the Bridegroom King Jesus, as He had called me to do.

Chapter 6

# *Bridal Dress Adventures*

IN THE MEANTIME, THE Holy Spirit would take me on trips to bridal shops. I would go in and look at hundreds of different types of bridal gowns. Each gown had its own beauty, and many had exquisite detail. Some of them had gold threads woven into the cloth, and others had threads of silver. Some were embellished with pearls and some with sequins, hearts, roses, lace, crystals or many other beautiful things.

Some wedding gowns were very tailored and simplistic, while others were full ball-like gowns of the Cinderella type. Still others were long, trained, and sleek — mermaid style. There were different materials for each dress, but all that I looked at were magnificent. When the right Bride put these dresses on, she would be perfection!

As the Holy Spirit was taking me to the bridal shops to show me all of this, He was also speaking to me from the Scriptures so that I could understand it all. For instance, He showed me:

**Psalm 45:13-14 (One New Man)**

*The king's daughter is all glorious within, her clothing is interwoven with gold; she will be led to the King in embroidered work.*

During the times I was shut in with the Holy Spirit, I again was in deep prayer. It was on one of those days that I had the vision of a book. Upon looking closer, I saw the glory of God all around it and within. I said to the Lord, "This must be your Holy Word."

It was then that He answered, "Elaine, this is the book you will write for Me, and it will be perfectly illustrated. The name of the book is *Threads of Gold.*"

Subsequently I discovered this phrase in Psalm 45:14: "*She will be led to the King in embroidered work [threads of gold]*" (One New Man).

Gold represents divinity, so His divine nature and the character of *Yeshua* will be used for the embroidery threads of our beautiful bridal robe — if we accept the work of the Holy Spirit, who holds the needle to do the piercing and if we allow Him to thread His own image into us, creating His imagine and likeness within us. He is Light, and He creates a covering of light for His Bride. The Father, in His nature, is also Light. Jesus Christ, as well, is the most pure and perfect embodiment of divine Light.

In Anna Roundtree's book, *The Priestly Bride,* she describes an embroidered robe: "It was full length with long sleeves. The design of the garment was simple. A man or woman could have worn it. Its richness lay in the embroidered work that was executed in white gold of exceptional purity. The embroidery arose from the robe. The pattern was intricate and exceptionally beautiful. As I moved a little before the garment, all the colors within the radiance of the Father seemed to play across its surface.

"The weight and thickness of the various gold threads seemed to symbolize attributes of the Lord. The robe reflected these as if they had been woven into the garment. I had no idea a garment could communicate that which was of the character of Christ.

"Still, I wanted to move slightly before the embroidery to ascertain what was woven into the fabric. I received the impression of a heart of compassion, kindness, humility, gentleness, and patience. The garment also reflected 'bearing with one another' and 'forgiving one another.' The thread that had the greatest weight and was the most frequently used was love."

"In Colossians 3:12 and 14, Paul tells the members of the Body of Christ to *put on* this garment. Jesus spoke to me and said, 'The garment is for the soul and heart. It is an inner garment that becomes visible through actions, and through decisions that effect unity (oneness in Christ).' He continued, 'I am the new, inner garment (and others rather than self). Clothe yourself in Me (with attributes of righteousness that are beautiful to God the Father).' The Lord's virtues woven into the garment had brought the Body of Christ into the perfect bond of unity. ... The embroidered garment is to be worn by those who are the Bride." [1]

How exciting it was to be part of something so meaningful!

Part II

# Threads Stretching from Childhood

Chapter 7

# Surrendering to God's Will

I SURRENDERED TO GOD'S will at a very young age. At the time, I didn't recognize it as Abba's will, but as I grew up, I recognized that it was from Him.

My life had not gotten off to a very good start. Just as God took Joseph from his father's house, He also took me from mine. I was born in Kansas City, but when my natural father came home one day and found me as a baby under a year old in neglected circumstances and my young mother unable to properly care for me, he decided to take me to a safe and caring place. This one act of love was and still is accredited to his honor to this day. You see, he had to surrender his will first.

My dad took me by train to my aunt's home in New Orleans where I could live and be safe. Mom and Dad were separated and getting a divorce, and he, out of love, wanted me to be provided for, but mostly to be wanted. He had called ahead and asked my aunt and uncle if they wanted me? They had two children of their own already. Why take someone else's baby? But God had chosen and, like Joseph, I was to grow up in the house God put me in. I would have to forget my father, my mother, my father's house, my father's face, my father's embrace, my father's name, my father's shame, my father's blame, my father's pain. And I did forget. I became very much the child of my new parents, my aunt and uncle.

**Psalm 45:10-11**

> *Listen O daughter, consider and give ear;*
> *Forget your people and your father's house.*

*"Forget your people."* It has always intrigued me that while reading someone's life story, you can read a few words in seconds, but the reality of those words can be a lifetime of hurt and healing. *Forget your people.* Those are just three words. And *"your father's house,"* another three words. We run them quickly through our lips like water rushing down a hill, but, oh my, believe me, living them does not rush by as quickly or as easily. Furiously, perhaps.

Sometimes for me to forget meant for me to be forgotten, but I would not be the first or only Bride to be asked to forget or surrender. It happened to Rebekah. She was asked if she would be willing (a surrendered will) to leave her people and her father's house to marry Isaac, Abraham's heir (see Genesis 24). She *was* willing, but when the time came, her brother and mother had a different response:

**42**

**Genesis 24:55**

> *But her brother and her mother replied, "Let the girl remain with us ten days or so; then you may go."*

Again, they are just three little words — *"you may go"* — but they are so very powerful.

The servant Abraham had sent to find a suitable bride for Isaac was not happy with this potential delay in something he knew to be so important:

**Genesis 24:56**

> *But he said to them, "Do not detain me, now that the LORD has granted success to my journey. Send me on my way so I may go to my master."*

They finally proposed asking Rebekah herself:

**Genesis 24:57**

> *Then they said, "Let's call the girl and ask her about it."*

So that was what they did, and they may have been surprised by her simple answer:

**Genesis 24:58**

> *So they called Rebekah and asked her, "Will you go with this man?"*
> *"I will go," she said.*

Three simple words again — *I will go*.

After my natural father had taken me to live with my aunt and uncle in New Orleans, I remained in their home for the next thirteen years. I was wanted by them. I was cared for by them. I was with them and among them, but I was not really one of them. I felt loved, but I was still lonely, as if I somehow didn't really belong.

I call the years I lived with my aunt and uncle my Moses-in-the-bulrushes days. Moses was being hidden from the enemy, and he was safely hidden away with Yahweh ... until it was his time to emerge. God knew what He was doing.

And so it was with me. I never saw my father again, but there I was growing in the safe place he had provided for me.

In the early years of my growing up in New Orleans, I wasn't consciously aware that I didn't really belong to that family. I believed that those were my parents and those were my siblings. I even went by their last name, and upon starting elementary school, I was called by that name. I wrote it on all my school work, and that's what my teachers, my friends, and even the members of our local church called me. So I was pretty secure in my identity — or so I thought.

Chapter 8

# Meeting Jesus

AT THE AGE OF eight I already had a hunger to know God. I mean I was on a mission to find Him. Our family attended a local Southern Baptist Church at the time, and I loved going to church, hearing the preaching and teaching, and learning all I could about Jesus. I couldn't wait until Sunday came around again so that I could go to Sunday school and learn more.

Looking back on it now, I can see that this is not the norm for most eight-year-olds. I was blessed at an early age to have a hunger for the Almighty.

**Song of Songs 1:4 (AMP)**
*Draw me! We will run after you!*

God was drawing me, and I was seeking Him. His Word declares:

**Jeremiah 29:13**

> *You will seek me and find me when you seek me with all your heart.*

**Psalm 27:8**

> *My heart says of you, "Seek his face!"*
> *Your face, Lord, I will seek*

**Psalm 27:9 (KJV)**

> *Thou hast been my help [aid, assist]; leave me not, neither forsake me, O God [Elohim] of my salvation. ...*
> *When my father and my mother forsake [abandon] me, then the Lord [Jehovah] will take me up [receive and protect me with all His saints].*

Shepherds gather the sheep in their arms, and this is what Jesus did for me.

At that tender age of eight, I was kneeling one night beside my bunk bed in the dark praying while everyone else in the house was already asleep. I remember praying but not exactly what I prayed. As I cried out in childlike faith, it happened: Abba God took me up. I saw in a vision, or picture, the following:

Jesus was on the cross, and I was kneeling before Him at the front of the cross looking up into His face. Then I was

Meeting Jesus

crying out with all my heart and soul to Jesus. "Please," I said, "please let me be on that cross, not You. I am the guilty one. I am a sinner. I deserve to be punished for my sins, not You."

I was brokenhearted, and as I cried, I remember trying my best to take Jesus off of the cross, saying over and over, "You did no wrong. You don't deserve this. I do. I'm the sinner."

I felt the weight of being a sinner, and I felt His holiness and compassion, but, mostly, I felt His love for me.

As I struggled with this, the Lord Jesus simply looked at me with those eyes. He said, "It's a free gift, Elaine. Just receive by grace. Just receive." In that moment, I felt the divine exchange. He took my place. By grace, I received the gift of salvation Jesus had purchased for me. It was free for me, but it was costly for Him. I received His forgiveness. All I sensed now from His presence was love and acceptance, and I surrendered my life to Him. He gave me His life, and He was now my Savior and Lord.

Many years later, when I was older, I learned that what had taken place in that moment was the revelation and act of *propitiation*. This word means "atonement, appeasement, or gift."

I felt the greatness of God's love. As John wrote to the Church:

**1 John 4:10 and 19 (AMP)**

> *In this is love, not that we loved God, but that*
> *He loved us and sent His Son to be the propitia-*
> *tion (the atoning sacrifice) for our sins.*
> *We love Him, because He first loved us.*

God's timing is perfect. I now belonged to Him.

Chapter 9

# A Blow to My Self-Esteem

TWO YEARS AFTER I was saved school authorities somehow learned that I was not a legal child of my aunt and uncle, and my guardians were informed that I could no longer use their name. It would be required, from then on, that I use my legal or given name (Marshall). It was a very difficult task for my beloved aunt and uncle to tell me about my false identity. In their hearts, they said, I was still their daughter, and they were still my family, but legally I could no longer use their name.

My name was now changed, and my security was shaken as a result. As a small child, I started asking, "Who do I belong to?" and "Where are my real mother and father?" More than any other question, I asked, "Why was I separated from them in the first place?" Inwardly I thought, "What is so wrong with me that even my own parents couldn't stand to be with me? What is so wrong with me that they didn't love me?"

I know without a doubt that this truth about my identity being changed was not allowed to come forth until I was saved and knew I already belonged to Jesus. This is what I mean by God always being on time. His timing is perfect. It was being loved by the Lord Jesus for two years prior to this announcement that helped me begin to accept the fact that I had been abandoned. And, even though I had been abandoned, I now had a new family and a new heavenly Father.

Unfortunately, being so young, I struggled with a spirit of rejection for many years because of this trauma. After all, in a child's mind, you must be "damaged goods" for your own mother and father not to want you and not to come and find you and claim you for so many years. What got me through this fiery trial was supernaturally devouring the Word of God. I would read the Bible (the best I could) and even other books and commentaries beyond my years. This was supernatural and not normal for a child of my age, but I was so hungry to know all about my loving Lord that I was driven to do it. My soul longed for Him.

My aunt and I would sit in the living room on the couch, and I would ask her questions for hours about the Bible. My friends and the cousins I lived with would want me to come outside and play with them, but I preferred to study the Bible and learn more about Jesus. This, of course, thrilled my aunt (whom I called Mama). She taught me all she could, but I always wanted more.

I am very thankful for those foundational years I had in the Baptist Church because it was there that I learned to love the Word and the God of the Word. The Holy Spirit was laying a sure foundation in my young and hungry heart.

**Isaiah 28:16**

> *So this is what the Sovereign LORD says:*
>
> *"See, I lay a stone in Zion, a tested stone,*
> *a precious cornerstone for a sure foundation;*
> *the one who trusts will never be dismayed."*

I wanted more! He had promised:

**Psalm 37:4**

> *Delight yourself in the LORD,*
> *and he will give you the desires of your heart.*

**Psalm 20:4**

> *May he give you the desire of your heart,*
> *and may all your plans succeed.*

I was determined to do my part to see those godly desires fulfilled.

Chapter 10

# A Suddenly

I LOVED GOING TO church, not only on Sundays, but whenever I could attend anything for my age group. On Wednesday afternoons our church offered the young people of my age and older a program called the GA's. It stood for Girl's Auxiliary, and there was one for the boys too. In the GA's there was a program you could do called Steps in which you were given a lot of scripture to memorize: like Psalms 1, 23, and 100, the Beatitudes and the Lord's Prayer, etc. As you progressed into more advanced steps, they became more difficult or age-appropriate. Each step took months to finish, and the whole program took years to complete, depending on how far you wanted to go.

The more difficult steps called for us to trace all of Paul's missionary journeys and memorize chapters and verses regarding them. I can't remember all the names of the various steps, but some of them were: "Lady-In Waiting," "Princess," "Queen," "Queen With a Scepter," etc. The highest step you could reach was "Queen in Regent," and she was the Bride. How I enjoyed working on those Bible projects and learning more about my Lord.

At the end of each quarter, the church would put on a pageant, and the girls of the GA would recite what they had memorized. Each of us would dress as pretty as we could to receive our awards. Following that ceremony there would be a celebration with food, cake, punch, and fellowship. For me, this was a very big deal. I loved it and looked forward each year to accomplishing the steps I was working on, so that I could advance to the next level.

One day, when I was twelve, four years after I was saved and two years after I had gone through the ordeal of learning my true identity, it seemed like a typical Wednesday afternoon. I went into the small building next to the church's main sanctuary, a room that was used for Sunday school classes, fellowship meetings, and children and youth gatherings. Our group was not large that day, just a few of us girls and an elderly teacher named Ms. White, and we were following one of Paul's missionary journeys.

Each of us was working on our own at the time, and no one was talking, but I distinctly heard someone call my name. I looked around, and when I didn't see anyone, I got up from my seat and went to Ms. White and asked her, "Did you call me?"

She said, "No," so I sat back down and continued to work on my project.

After a little while, I again heard someone calling, "Elaine."

I got up again and went to the teacher and said, "You wanted me? You called my name"?

"No," she said, "go sit down, honey" So I did.

The third time I clearly heard someone calling me by name I said nothing. Instead, I felt impressed to get up and leave the room. I got up quietly and went outside, but still I didn't know what to do. I just waited a little while, and then I was led to go next door to the sanctuary.

As I entered the main sanctuary of the church, I was led by the Holy Spirit to go up the steps onto the platform, where the pastor usually sat and from where he preached, and I stood in front of the choir loft and waited and waited some more.

I was not sure what I was waiting for, but then, suddenly, a presence, an anointing came mightily upon me, and the whole atmosphere changed. I could tangibly feel a weight coming over me and resting upon me, as if a cloak had been dropped onto my shoulders. Then my spiritual eyes were opened.

As this was happening, I had no understanding of what it all meant. But when my spiritual eyes were opened, I saw that a long robe, or garment, had been placed upon me. It stretched from my shoulders to the floor, and I immediately felt like "Queen for a Day."

Then I saw Jesus standing next to me, and I said to Him, "Lord, this is too big for me."

He said, "You will learn and grow into it. I will help you."

Looking into Jesus' face and eyes brought to me a calm assurance and faith that He would do as He had promised.

I was quite small for my age, and I felt overwhelmed by the garment, or mantle, that had been placed on me. But it was a beautiful garment, although it was simple, not terribly ornate. It had many colors in its various folds, making me think of Joseph's coat of many colors. But these colors were hidden in the folds, not visible when looking at it straight on.

There were also silver and gold threads throughout, and yet these, too, were not prominent to the eye. The beauty of the garment was somehow hidden, and this gave it the appearance of being simple.

I then saw some men standing before me from five different nations, and the Lord said, "You will be with these five men in your lifetime. You will give them help and receive wisdom in return. Remember, this is part of your destiny." And, with that, the Lord was gone.

I began to pace back and forth behind the pulpit, and all the while, I was prophesying and preaching. I had never ever heard anyone prophesy before (for it was not permitted in our Southern Baptist churches). This was a sovereign act of God.

I'm not sure how long I prophesied, but after a certain amount of time, I came out from under that anointing and looked around. Sitting there in the upper balcony of the church was the entire group of girls from the GAs, my older cousin, and the teacher. As they came down and got closer to me, I could see that they were all weeping. Tears streamed down their faces, and yet I could see joy and smiles on their faces.

My cousin and the teacher looked at me and asked, "How did you learn to do this?"

I answered, "I don't know," and I didn't. I was beginning to experience God on a new level.

Chapter 11

# *The Appearance of a Strange Lady*

THE SUMMER BEFORE I entered Junior High School (seventh grade), our whole family gathered around the kitchen table one evening to plan our vacation. The atmosphere was full of excitement. Maps and tourist brochures were laid out for all to see, and we were deciding where we wanted to go and what we wanted to do. Finally, we had our plans made, and the dates were set and marked on the calendar.

Suddenly, we heard a car drive up in front of the house. It was unfamiliar to us, and we wondered who might be coming. A strange woman got out and walked toward the house. Keep in mind that I had lived with my aunt and uncle (whom I called Mama and Daddy) since I was a baby. My aunt (Mama) now went to answer the knock at the door.

When she opened the door, she was surprised to see her older sister Dee standing there. They hadn't seen each other in many years. Dee was invited into the house, and all the kids crowded around to meet her. "This is my sister Dee, your aunt," Mama said to us.

Then she looked specifically at me. "Elaine," she said, "come over here … closer. This is your mother."

My "mother?" I already had a mother, one that I had lived with since I could remember anything. At that moment, everything moved into slow motion. This person in front of me was a total stranger. How could she be my mother?

The other children were excited to meet Dee, their new aunt, and make her feel welcome. She said she could stay for a week. We didn't have room for her to sleep with us, so she said she would stay at the Fontainebleau Hotel, and over that next week we began to get acquainted.

My sister (cousin) and I went over to the Fontainebleau to swim in the pool often, and we had a good time, but somehow Dee remained a complete stranger to me. All I could think about was when this unexpected visit would be over so that we could get back to being happy about our upcoming vacation plans.

I was an outgoing child, not shy, so Dee (my mom) and I could easily talk. I discovered that her visit had not been all that much of a surprise. She had informed my aunt (Mama) that she would be coming. This surprised me, and I believe my aunt (Mama) thought or hoped that her sister might change her mind and not come after all. She had threatened to just show up on other occasions, and had always had a last-minute change of plans. Not so this time around. Here she was. Now what?

Each night, when we had all gone to bed, I could hear the other children discussing something loudly among themselves, but I could never make out the topic of their conversations. Something mysterious was in the air.

Chapter 12

# A Trip to California

THE END OF THE week finally arrived, when Dee would be leaving. I was relieved. Then my cousin (sister) and I were called to come and sit down beside my aunt (Mama), and I wondered what was up. There was something tense in the atmosphere again. She asked, "How would the two of you like to fly with my sister Dee to California for a couple of weeks?"

Dee chimed in with all the exciting places we could visit if we accompanied her to California for those weeks, places like Disneyland and Seaworld. It did sound exciting, and it would be our first plane trip, but I was frightened by the prospect and kept telling my cousin (sister) that I really didn't want to go. She kept reassuring me nothing bad could happen; we would always be together. I worried that we would miss our family vacation, but everyone assured me we would return in plenty of time. We would be going on a round-trip ticket with precise return dates. Eventually we agreed, and the three of us — Dee, my sister, and I — flew to California, and Dee showed us a good time, as promised.

Dee lived in a lovely home in Chatsworth. It had a beautiful in-ground pool, and every morning we got up and immediately headed for that pool. I even learned how to high dive. Although long-distance calls were still quite expensive, we were able to speak with our family back home in New Orleans, and that was a treat for us.

As the two weeks were coming to an end, and it was time for us to pack our bags and board the plane home, both my sister and I were very excited. It would be such fun to get back home and share our adventures with the rest of the family. And we were looking forward to our next adventure with them.

We went to ask Dee if we could use her phone to call home and give them the details of our flight arrival and were surprised when she said, "No, it costs too much." Then she added, "And, anyway, things had changed."

"What has changed?" we asked. Dee then told us that my aunt (Mama) had agreed for me to stay on longer, until the end of the summer. My sister would go home as planned, but she would be going alone.

We were stunned! I began crying and saying to my sister, "Please don't leave me here by myself, I want to go home with you." She tried to comfort me by saying, "Mama and Daddy would never agree to leave you here. They will make Dee send you home."

We went to Dee and begged her to let us make a call home and reverse the charges. This isn't done much anymore, but it meant that the person receiving the call paid for it. We thought this would remove her objection to the call on the basis of cost, but she objected nonetheless.

Later that evening, Dee picked up the phone and pretended to be calling our parents and telling them that I had agreed to stay the rest of the summer. She was lying on two counts: (1) She didn't call anyone, and (2) I had not agreed to stay with her. I was not about to miss that wonderful family vacation. She knew this, but chose to deceive everyone. All I could do was cry in my sister's arms that night.

Dee did let me go with them to the airport, but it was a very traumatic experience. Mom objected. After all, she said, we would be reunited in a few months. My sister disappeared, and I was left alone with Dee and another stranger — her fourth husband. He rarely uttered a word.

Later that evening we got a long-distance call from New Orleans. It was Mama. Dee didn't answer it. When Mama had gone to the airport to pick us up, and only my sister appeared, she immediately asked, "Where is your sister Laney (my nickname at the time)?"

"What do you mean, where is she?" my sister replied, "You allowed her to stay with Dee the rest of the summer." Mama was shocked by this and suddenly realized that she had been betrayed by her own sister. She immediately began trying to call Dee by phone, but there was no response (and there were no cell phones in those days).

In New Orleans, everyone began to panic. What should they do? What *could* they do? They were poor and didn't have money to buy a plane ticket to fly out and rescue me. And Mama had a three-month-old baby who needed her attention. All she knew to do was to pray and hope that she would hear from me soon.

Chapter 13

# Realizing I Had Been Kidnapped

MEANWHILE, IN CALIFORNIA, THE relationship between Dee and me was cold and distant. I could hardly bring myself to speak to her because of her betrayal. I knew in my heart that I had been kidnapped and was being held against my will and my family's will for me. And the worst part was that I had no way of escape.

Things were so bad between us that Dee wrote me a letter explaining that it was her turn to be with me after a lifetime of absence. She said that if her sister tried to get me back, she would take them to court, and, as my birth mother, she was sure she would win. She said she deserved a chance to spend time with me and threatened my parents that if they tried to come and take me back, she would move somewhere even further away, and they would never see me again.

Because of these threats, my parents agreed for me to stay with Dee the rest of the summer, but I must be returned home in time for the new school term. That never happened. At the end of the summer Dee told me she was taking me to enroll in a nearby school. I would be staying with her indefinitely.

Upon hearing this news, I decided to take matters into my own hands. One way or another, I was going home. That night, when they were asleep, I quietly slipped out of the house and walked to a nearby highway, where I began to try to hitch a ride with passing cars. No one stopped. I was a young teenager, and it was late at night and I was alone, but no one offered me a ride.

Then, after quite awhile, a police car pulled up alongside me and asked me where was I going and why? The officer insisted on taking me back "home." He told Dee and her husband that he had found me hitch-hiking on a major highway and expressed how dangerous that was for me. They were shocked, expressed their sorrow at the whole affair, and urged the officer not to file charges against me. When the officer had gone, I was beaten with a belt by Dee's husband (apparently my new step-dad). It would not be the last time.

But I didn't give up that easily. This conduct went on for awhile, me leaving in the middle of the night, then being found and brought back to Dee's house, and punished again. I guess they thought fear would eventually make me decide to stay. It didn't.

Just before I started school, they did allow me to call and talk to my family in New Orleans one time. Mama said they were saving their money to send my brother (cousin) to come out and bring me back home. This encouraged me. I found new strength and decided to play along with Dee and my step-dad. Mama's words had given me hope that one day I would be rescued.

Eventually, at the end of that school year, my brother (cousin) did come to California by bus to get me. He had just graduated from high school and was then eighteen or nineteen, but he was no match for Dee. He had come determined to take me back home, but he was daily bombarded with threats and intimidation. He resisted this as long as he could, but eventually accepted defeat and went home empty handed. I felt so sorry for him.

Chapter 14

# *Left Unprotected*

DEE WAS STILL BASKING in her triumph, having won me as her prize, when suddenly she left my step-dad and me and moved to Las Vegas to be with another man. She apparently hadn't wanted me all that bad; she just didn't want anyone else to have me. Now, as usual, she was free to live her life as she pleased. Being a mother had never been part of her plan, and all along I had been treated more like an object than a real person.

Needless to say, the arrangement between my step-dad and me didn't go well. He was very angry with Dee, but she was gone, and I was still there, so he began to take out his frustrations on me. He was a construction worker and had developed very strong arms in his work, and I weighed less than a hundred pounds. He would work himself into a rage and then come after me with his belt. Some days, after one of those beatings, I would have to stay home from school until the bruises and welts had healed. He was afraid he might be turned in for child abuse if someone saw me during gym class.

Dee would occasionally come home for a weekend visit (it wasn't a long drive from Las Vegas to Los Angeles. She saw the bruises and welts once and got into a big fight with my step-dad. But then, as usual, she left again and went back to her life. It always puzzled me why she had kidnapped me in the first place if she didn't really love me and want me. Why bother to go through all of that, just to leave me? Later, I figured out that it was more of a control issue.

Obviously, both Dee and my step-dad were lost. Neither of them knew the Lord, and I was the only witness in their lives at that time.

Things did change for me some after Dee threatened my step-dad about the physical abuse, but the change was for the worse. Shortly after she left to go back to Las Vegas to be with her new lover, my step-dad, suffering low self-esteem because his wife was living with another man, and he was stuck at home with her daughter, got drunk and came into my bedroom.

He had his belt in hand, and it seemed, at first, like just his normal rage, but then it went much further. He began trying to rape me. I was still thirteen. If I resisted him, he would beat me much harder. Things went on this way until he said to me one day, "We can do this one of two ways: (1) Either we can do this without beatings, or (2) With beatings, but we *will* do this regardless." I resigned myself to the inevitable, sure that I would be saved as soon as Dee learned what was happening. She would kick him out or have him arrested.

I told him my plan, to tell her that he was raping me now, as well as abusing me often, thinking that this would frighten him enough to make him stop or perhaps leave. But all it accomplished was to give him reason to laugh at me and mock me more. "Go ahead and tell your mom," he said. "She won't believe your word over mine. I've been married to her seven years, and you've been with her only one. She'll throw you out into the streets, and you will be homeless and forsaken."

That night I remember standing at my bedroom window, looking out at the stars and praying: "Father God, I am Your child, and someone is abusing me. Please come and protect me. No one else will or can stop this treatment toward me. You, Father, are all I have. No one else cares about my life. Tell me what to do."

Chapter 15

# Father God Rescues Me

I HAD ASKED GOD to help me and tell me what to do, and He did. The next time my step-dad came to my bedroom to beat and rape me, he was in for a big surprise. I was waiting for him outside the bedroom door, and I had a new confidence. I told him that Father God had told me that if he ever tried to cross over the threshold of my room to do evil again he would regret it and meet resistance. I declared that I was supernaturally protected by angels and that they were more powerful than he.

"It is finished!" I said, and the fear of the Lord came over his face, and his entire body began to tremble (just as I had often trembled with fear of him). He laughed awkwardly but turned and went back down the hallway. He never again returned to my bedroom or any other room with a belt in his hand or with evil in his eyes, and he never raped me again.

Gradually his health began to decline, and he was diagnosed, just a few months later, with terminal lung cancer.

He moved out of the house and went back to live with his mother, while he underwent chemotherapy and radiation treatments. When he became too weak to undergo any more treatments, he asked Dee if he could come back and live with us in that house. She felt guilty for the way she had treated him, and so she allowed him to stay in a small apartment there.

It was evident that he was going downhill quickly. A few weeks before his death the Holy Spirit told me I needed to forgive him for raping me and for the rest of his abuse. I began to pray for his salvation.

When he became very weak and was hospitalized, I went to his room and prayed with him. He asked for forgiveness and prayed the sinner's prayer. He said to me, "If you can forgive me, after all I have done to you, it must come from God. The power to do that can only come from God." His face was shining with the light of Yahweh on it. Great grace had been poured into me to forgive him, and it was just in time. He didn't have much time to live.

Just before Thanksgiving, Dee and I went to the hospital at midnight, after all the patients had been put to sleep for the night. All was quiet. I stood by his bedside, stroking his forehead and telling him how much he was loved by his heavenly Father and his family. We would be taking him home in the morning via ambulance so that he could enjoy Thanksgiving dinner. After praying with him, I kissed him, said good night, and we went to a nearby motel to sleep. In the middle of the night, the phone rang, and immediately we knew that it must be bad news. It was the ICU nurse saying that my step-dad had died. His fight was over, and he had found peace. I was glad.

"How could you forgive him?" some ask. Our Lord Jesus teaches us that love does not keep score. God is Love, and He is the great Accountant. He alone will bring balance to the scales of injustice in our lives. Through His intervention, a story of rape and abuse had become a story of rescue and redemption.

Chapter 16

# Restoring My Dignity

I HAVE READ THAT A child needs dignity, and after being violated, I needed my dignity restored. I needed to hear that someone was proud of me. Oddly I had never heard those words spoken by the parents who raised me. I had been orphaned just as much as if I had been in some third-world and never had human contact. There is more than one way to orphan a child, and I experienced most of them.

One way is to be non-affectionate, and another is to show improper sexual affections. Another way is through neglect, to be cold and distant. Another is to never allow the child to be heard or have a voice, causing their words to never carry weight with other people. Some of these I experienced during this time of an absentee mother and an abusive step-dad.

The enemy offered me one of his specialty garments to wear. It was called Shame, and with Shame there comes a sense of being completely insufficient as a person. I was left with a nagging feeling that for some reason I was defective, unworthy, and damaged goods. On top of that, when proof of abuse, neglect, or abandonment is given, and you are not believed, that's many times worse.

During those years of being abandoned by my birth mom, I lived in terror, and for a child, terror is measured in seconds, not minutes, days, or months. You live your life constantly holding your breath.

Shame suffocates you. It makes you stand on high alert, asking yourself, "Will I be left alone tonight? Or will I hear the jingling of that dreaded belt?" I was traumatized by that sound, and this continued until after I was married. My husband could be dressing in another room, and I would feel that same fear coming over me immediately upon hearing him put on or take off his belt. One day he witnessed my strong reaction, and I finally confessed to him why I became so fearful when I heard the sound of a belt buckle.

I have learned that traumas that are denied can never be healed. When we bring them into the light, they lose their power.

Jesus said, *"Blessed are they that mourn: for they shall be comforted"* (Matthew 5:4, KJV). It is good to mourn over the loss of dignity, innocence, being heard and believed, and much more. This is why the Father Abba sent his Holy Spirit as the Comforter and also people we can trust to draw us close to Him.

In my adult years, I was determined to get healed from all these wounds and delivered from the pain and anger. I have read and agree that if we don't learn to transform the pain, we'll transfer it. This is one of the reasons I write this book, because it is by the word of my testimony and by the blood of the Lamb that I overcome (see Revelation 12:11).

I hold on to the promise of my Abba God in my heart. In John 14:18, He says: *"I will not leave you as orphans; I will come to you."* When I felt all alone in my baby crib and was deprived of basic needs, such as soiled diapers changed and milk in my bottle, not to mention the lack of nurturing, minimal physical human contact, being starved for affection, the brain and body learn to disconnect from their surroundings. This carried on into my teen years and I was able to disconnect my emotions while being violated and abused for survival. I did the best I could.

What kept me from perishing totally? I knew that Jesus loved me unconditionally. The first scripture I ever learned was this:

### John 3:16 (KJV)

*For God [ABBA] so loved the world [and me], that he gave [not took] his only begotten Son, that whosoever believeth [relies and trusts] in him should not perish [give up], but have everlasting life.*

Only the power of the Word and the Holy Spirit can transform you and me from being orphans (the lowest place) to queens (the highest place). I am now His Queen of Hearts.

The reason I could overcome these and other events in my life was that I had met my Redeemer and heard Him tell me my destiny. To be a lily among the thorns is to wear the cloak of humility given to me by the Lord and to go low and stay low. I had to learn experientially how to forgive my enemies and bless those who persecuted me.

The gold thread of "Love never fails" was being woven over and over into my wedding garment. I have done my best to glorify the goodness of the Lord to me during this season of my life and give the enemy none. This is part of my redeeming love story:

1. Jesus redeemed me to be a spiritual mother to others, as well as a natural mother and grandmother with great grace.
2. He redeemed me to trust my husband and enjoy intimacy with him.
3. He redeemed me to forgive people who betray me.
4. He redeemed me to never be ashamed again.

He was preparing me to be the Bride of Christ.

Chapter 17

# Receiving My Coat of Many Colors

AFTER SEVERAL YEARS OF separation from my family because of the kidnapping, I finally saw them again, at my grandmother's farm in Kansas.

The kidnapping had caused a terrible rift in the family, and so after a few years (I was sixteen at the time) Grandma asked our two families to come to meet again on neutral ground at her place. Mom would never have allowed me to go alone, for fear I would go back to live with my New Orleans family, but she did agree to go with me to this family gathering. I was very excited to see everyone again, but I was constantly under Mom's watchful eye.

My aunt, my cousins, and a new sister-in-law all came to the farm. I knew the girl who had married my oldest cousin (the same cousin who had been sent to California to bring me home and was unable to). Surprisingly, all during that visit, no one ever spoke about the kidnapping or its aftermath. I remember being frequently hugged by my aunt and reassured that I was still loved and missed, but she didn't try to pull me away from my mother.

I didn't stay in Kansas that time only because I had just one more year of high school to finish before I graduated. Mom knew that, and I'm sure that's why she agreed to the visit. She was now in and out of my life because she frequently went to New York City (with her new male friend). She wanted me to leave high school and live with them, but I refused. I felt I needed some roots and stability in my life, and I couldn't get that living with her. She would fly out sometimes for a weekend.

Mom and I had come to a mutual standoff. There was no real love or warmth between us. This didn't come until much later, after I had been diagnosed with breast cancer, and the Lord told me it was from harboring unforgiveness toward her and that I needed to forgive her of everything she had done to hurt me.

I feel sure that the farm meeting had been called for my benefit and the sake of my New Orleans family, so that we could see and hold each other again, and prior to going, we all agreed to lay down our bitterness and come together for old time's sake. The hardest part was when it came time to leave again. Saying goodbye this time was doubly difficult because now it looked as if I was choosing to be with my mom rather than with them. Later my aunt comforted me in this regard. I wrote and told her that I felt guilty for not having put up more of a fight, but she answered that it had been the right thing to do at the time.

Later, after I had married, my husband and I went to New Orleans many times to see my family there. Both my aunt and uncle have passed away now, but I was grateful to them for the kindnesses they showed me in those early years of my life.

As for Mom, her life was like the woman Jesus met at the well. She had five husbands, and then she met the Master. Mom told me that when she surrendered her life to the Lord it was because she had seen how I was able to forgive her. That grace and strength, she knew, had to come from the Lord. I consider the restoration of my relationship to my mother and her salvation my greatest miracle (and I have experienced many).

There was another important thing about the farm meeting. It was Grandma's habit to knit each of her grandchildren an afghan, and when it came to mine, she made it from the remnants left over from other yarns. Therefore it was multi-colored, like Joseph's coat of many colors. At the tender age of sixteen, when I received that afghan, I saw it as a symbol of the remnant Bride. Not only was it made from remnants, but it also had threads of gold woven throughout it.

Whether everyone else recognized it or not, I cannot say for sure, but God was weaving a glorious thread through my life.

Chapter 18

# Marriage and Children

SO I HAD BEEN BORN in Kansas, taken at less than a year old by my father to live with my aunt and uncle in New Orleans, and then kidnapped there at thirteen and forced to live with my mother and step-father in California. Not everything was loss for me there. Eventually I graduated from high school in Van Nuys.

Then, since my step-father had died from lung cancer, Mom and I moved to Las Vegas, Nevada. She had another male friend there. I went to nursing school, and she worked various jobs. After graduating from nursing school, I worked in a hospital in Las Vegas in the CCU (Cardiac Care Unit) and the ICU. During this time, I moved into my own apartment with a roommate.

That summer my roommate had a date one evening and called me from the Stardust Hotel to ask me to come meet her date's friend. That was my one and only blind date, and the man turned out to be my future husband, Roy Perry.

Roy was from Upstate New York and was attending Syracuse University. He had decided to come to Vegas with some friends for the summer. They soon ran out of money, and he got a part-time job and stayed on.

Roy and I dated for a year and then decided to get married, but we didn't want to stay in Las Vegas, feeling that it would not be a good place to raise a family. Neither of us gambled or had any desire to, and there was something about the spirit of the town that we didn't care for.

Roy wanted to go back and finish his college, and Mom had remarried (husband number five) to the personnel director of the Stardust Hotel, and they had decided to move to Kansas "to start over" and to be near my grandmother, who was ill at the time. So where should Roy and I settle?

From the beginning Roy had wanted to return to Upstate New York, but that seemed so very far away to me. I also didn't think I could stand the cold winters there. We finally met on that same neutral ground of Kansas. We were married in Kansas City and lived there for the next thirty-one years.

Roy became a construction manager, and, through the years, worked in a variety of construction jobs. Homes, malls, schools, and churches were among the things he built. In later years, he worked in historic preservation construction and won an award from the State of New York in that field.

Along the way God gave us three children, a daughter, Alison, and two sons, Matthew and Adam, and eventually eleven grandchildren. But this story is not about us; it's about what God was doing to reveal His Bride.

Chapter 19

# Discovering and Embracing My Jewish Roots

IT WAS ONLY AFTER going to live with my mother in California that I discovered my Jewish roots. Her dad was Jewish. I was thrilled by this revelation, and immediately embraced my Jewishness. I was a part of God's chosen people.

This realization gave way to a whole new set of revelations concerning what it means to be a Messianic Christian believer. I had for years loved the types and symbols of the Scripture, and now I knew why. They were a part of my DNA.

To this day, our family celebrates both Christian and Hebraic holidays. As I learned about Hebraic traditions concerning brides and marriage, my life was further enriched, and the Holy Spirit just kept giving me new insights into the Bride.

Chapter 20

# *Receiving the Baptism of the Holy Spirit*

IN THE 1980s, I received the baptism of the Holy Spirit in a Baptist church. I pressed in during a revival meeting and said to God, "I am not leaving here until You set me free, Jesus." I began crying, with tears flowing down my cheeks. I felt a tender touch on my face wiping the tears away and opened my yes to find my son Adam touching me.

I got up from my pew and went forward and knelt down at the altar. Then I literally felt a huge weight come off of me, as if a heavy chain had been wrapped around my being. Now I was crying tears of joy, and was so glad this was happening in front of the entire church (at least I thought they could see what was happening to me).

Next, the best I can describe it (words do not describe supernatural events well), I was picked up by the Lord

Jesus and baptized in liquid love. It was everywhere. Love was in my hair, around my face, inside me, in my mouth, in and around my whole body. I was immersed in this warm liquid love inside and out. It was so wonderful that I thought to myself, "I'm going to die!" My very next thought was: "Who cares if I die; I am with Jesus already."

All of my spiritual senses were quickened and came alive. My eyes could see Jesus, my ears could hear His voice, my mouth could taste and see the Lord's goodness, and my nose could smell His fragrance. I could feel Him, know Him, and commune with Him spirit to Spirit.

*"For in him we live and move and have our being"* (Acts 17:28) was now experiential, not just knowledge, not just words. I had been crying out to know Him on a deeper level. Although I had been saved, something had been missing. My daily bread had become Paul's prayer for the Ephesians:

**Ephesians 1:17-19**

*I keep asking that the God of our Lord Jesus Christ, the glorious Father, may give you the Spirit of wisdom and revelation, so that you may know him better. I pray also that the eyes of your heart may be enlightened in order that you may know the hope to which he has called you, the riches of his glorious inheritance in the saints, and his incomparably great power for us who believe.*

I had asked, over and over, to experience the Lord beyond knowledge, doctrine, or logic, to be one with Him.

Jesus said:

**John 4:24**

> *God is spirit, and his worshippers must worship in spirit and in truth.*

Now I could do this. With my own human spirit, I could participate with the Holy Spirit within me. His river was flowing through me and from me.

Before the baptism, my persona or spirit was encased and non-functioning in this area. After being baptized, everything came alive. Trees were greener. The sky was bluer. I loved myself and everyone around me. The future was going to be wonderful.

# Part III

# More Revelations on the Bride and Her Beloved

Chapter 21

# *The Necessary Longing*

**Song of Songs 7:10 (KJV)**

*I am my beloved's, and his desire is for me. [I am His Shulamite.]*

I WOKE UP EARLY one morning to hear this word in my spirit — *longing*. Even in hearing the word I sensed the emotion. It was G.K. Chesterton, an English writer, who spoke of "the furious love of God." He was referring to the enormous vitality and strength of the Abba of Yeshua seeking union with us.

*Fury* means "an intense energy." The emotion I first sensed was aching to know God, to know Abba.

He also aches to know us. He longs for us. Abba is longing for you and me right now. Longing is His gift to us.

When I say that I was aching to know Abba, people seem to automatically think it is because I don't already know Him. That is not the case. What I mean is that I long to know Him more deeply.

He longs for us furiously, with a deep emotion toward us. Jesus is longing to show us the Father.

I am invited to a feast, a wedding feast. We have all been invited to God's feast of furious love. I have personally been invited to His banqueting table, and His banner over me is love. He said:

**John 13:34 (KJV)**

*Love one another; as I have loved you.*

I hear the Lord saying:

*Come now, my Love, my Lovely one, come.*
*All it takes is surrender.*
*Be still and know that I am God!*

I love that old hymn of the church:

*All to Jesus I surrender.*
*All to Him I freely give.*
*I will always love and trust Him,*
*In His presence daily live.*

*I surrender all.*
*I surrender all.*

*All to Thee, my blessed Savior,*
*I surrender all.* [2]


Longing, the furious longing of God ... it means "a passionate, vehement craving."

Can you say, "Abba, I belong to You?"

He is saying to each of us, "You are mine."

Can we ever forget the powerful song we learned as children?

*Jesus loves me! This I know,*
*For the Bible tells me so;*
*Little ones [like me] to Him belong;*
*They are [I am] weak, but He is strong.*

*Yes, Jesus loves me.*
*Yes, Jesus loves me.*
*Yes, Jesus loves me.*
*The Bible tells me so.* [3]


I love this poem by my brother, Gary Weins of Kansas City:

*Longing*
*Lovely Lord, stretch forth, Your wounded hand,*
*And drip the precious, fragrant flow of passionate*
*love all over me again.*
*Retake my battered heart,*

> *Steal me away to the secret place,*
> *Where the deep and deep engage.* [4]

The Bride of Christ is like Joseph. He said:

**Genesis 41:51**

> *For God ... hath made me forget all my toil, and all*
> *my father's house.*

It took Joseph years to fully surrender his life. Submission is the response of love, the response to being loved.

One of the first gold threads in the Holy Spirit's needlework in my own robe was surrender or longing. I, too, had to forget my father's house.

Longing makes us willing for whatever life brings.

Chapter 22

# Longing and Fulfillment

**Matthew 5:6**

*Blessed are those who hunger and thirst for righteousness, for they will be filled.*

DANA CANDLER HAS WRITTEN, "Christ is both the longing and the fulfillment of love, the One who is Desire is also the One who is Satisfaction. Within Him are the wound and the healing. He provides the thirst that makes us desperate, and He provides the drink that satisfies. We partake of His longing, and we partake of His fulfillment. He desires that we would be with Him in love and union, satisfied forever in the eternal pleasure of His being.

"Our hearts cry out, 'O, God, I must have more of You! I must know You, even as I am known!' We only desire what He first desired. If He is the desire, will He not also be the Satisfier? If He is the Thirst, will He not also be the Water?

"We begin to hunger for the capacity to hunger. We begin to thirst for the ability to thirst. The longing to long is the escort into longing itself. It is the God-ordained gateway into the true gift of God, to crave Him with all of our beings. He carves us out and enlarges our capacity through hunger and desire, that He might fill us with Himself. Where there is divine longing, there is also divine fulfillment." [5]

An example of the Holy Spirit teaching me this was through my young son Adam back during the 1980s. He desperately wanted to get me something for my birthday, but, at just six years old, he had no money of his own. So he would look around the house and find something I liked, take it to his room, and wrap it up for me. Then, on my birthday, he would hand me that "present."

Of course, upon opening the gift, I would act surprised and say, "Oh, I *love* this. Thank you, honey." And he was happy because I was pleased. In the same way, the Lord first gives us the gifts of longing and hunger for more, and then He fills us with the satisfaction only He can give. As our Father, He, too, acts pleased with His own gifts.

# *Her Glorious Clothing*

**Psalm 45:11-13**

> *The King is enthralled by your beauty;*
> *honor him, for he is your lord.*
> *The Daughter of Tire will come with a gift,*
> *men of wealth will seek your favor.*
> *All glorious is the princess within her chamber;*
> *her gown is interwoven with gold.*

THIS PHRASE *INTERWOVEN WITH gold* is translated *"wrought" gold"* in the King James Version and *"inwrought gold"* in the Amplified. Women embroidered with gold thread.

**Ephesians 2:10**

> *For we are God's workmanship, created in Christ Jesus to do good works, which God prepared in advance for us to do.*

**1 Peter 5:5**

> *All of you, clothe yourselves with humility toward one another, because,*
>
> *God opposes the proud but gives grace to the humble.*

**Psalm 45:14a**

> *In embroidered garments she is led to the King [in raiment of needlework, embroidered robes or tapestry).*

This represents an interweaving of the variously-colored hues of ministry.

**Psalm 45:14b**

> *Her virgin companions follow her.*

The Bride's dress is also a type of Joseph's coat and the covenant rainbow promises of God.

Upon studying biblical color meanings, I read that the blends of multi-colors can stand for Jubilee, with all nations and tribes and the apostolic favor of the Lord. A rainbow of colors — red, orange, yellow, green, blue, and purple — can stand for the rainbow itself, God's covenant, the seal of God that gives hope and promise, or, in other words, His great promises.

Joseph was clothed with divine favor in a brilliant and outstanding coat of many colors. It was the symbol of

Yahweh's choice and purpose resting upon him, a symbol of his anointing.

The King James Version of the Bible renders this verse as follows:

> *The king's daughter is all glorious within: her clothing is of wrought gold.*

*"All glorious within"* ... that is *"Christ in you, the hope of glory"* (Colossians 1:27). So clothe yourselves with the Lord Jesus Christ (see Romans 13:4).

Chapter 24

# Her Awakening

**Song of Songs 8:5 (AMP)**

*Under the apple tree I awakened you.*

"*I*" ... JESUS IS THE Awakener.

"*You*" ... this includes all those who hunger for and desire only Him.

It is said that only God can love God. He is the Initiator. He gives to us the gift of an awakened heart, to then offer it back to Him. He is the Alpha and the Omega, the Beginning and the End. He is our All in All. It all begins with Him. He causes love to awaken.

Apples represent the Word of God, as in Proverbs 15:11:

**Proverbs 25:11 (KJV)**

*A word fitly spoken is like apples of gold in pictures of silver.*

Jesus is our Satisfaction and Shelter. He is our Apple tree and our Tree of Life, as Peter said in John 6:68:

**John 6:68**

> *"Lord, to whom shall we go? You have the words of eternal life."*

Chapter 25

# His Kiss

**Song of Songs 1:2**

> *Let him kiss me with the kisses of his mouth —*
> *for your love is more delightful than wine.*

*"KISS ME."* SHE ASKS for this kiss, and you, too, must ask to be kissed. He is waiting for you to ask.

The ultimate romance is God, a divine romance. The universe was created for love, and the purpose of your existence is love.

We are recipients of God's love. We were created by Love for Love, for God is Love. He is our Magnificent Obsession, the very Son of God.

*"Kiss me"* is the individual walk in the divine romance. You were created to satisfy God's heart above any other desire you may have.

*"Let."* This word shows submission to the Lord.

*"Kiss."* This word means "fasten, touch, attach, or equip with weapons." The king is calling us to heart love, for the mouth is the expression of the heart (see Matthew 12:34).

Jesus paid a high price, giving up His divinity to become human and giving up His life for you and me. Love is costly. Will you now surrender your life to Him?

Chapter 26

# Her Kiss

**Psalm 2:12**

*Kiss the Son.*

BUT HOW DO I kiss You, Yeshua?

In ancient times, the slave or serf would say to his or her lord, "I want to kiss you." This was significant. The lord would sit in a chair, and the slave would kneel between his legs. Then the lord would take a rope and, with the slaves hands crossed in front of him, wrap the rope around his hands.

Then the slave would say to his lord, "I give up my rights," meaning that he was surrendering his strength and will to his lord. So when you have given up every right to your Lord, you will have kissed Him. Kissing the Lord meant giving up strength, power, possessions, reputation, and rights or surrendering all.

Chapter 27

# *The Anointing of His Name*

**Song of Songs 1:3**

> *Pleasing is the fragrance of your perfumes;*
> *your name is like perfume poured out.*
> *No wonder the maidens [virgins] love you.*

THIS IS YESHUA'S ANOINTING, and there is a release of His anointing upon us as well. The virgins are primarily concerned with what He does and not who He is. His name is purified, but the virgins love the blessing more than the responsibility of the birthright. They are often overbalanced in one area of ministry. The possibilities of overbalance are without number.

**Song of Songs 6:8**

> *... and virgins beyond number ...*

The outer court is full of them. They love the gift more than the Giver of Grace.

At this point, the Bride is just one among many, but she is dissatisfied with the ordinary. Her eyes are beginning to open (see Ephesians 1:18), and she must have more.

Though her love is immature and self-centered, it is genuine. The King sees her, and He must do for her what she cannot do for herself. He must draw her:

> *Draw me, we will run after thee.*
> Song of Songs 1:4, KJV

She cries out, "*Your name is as perfume [to be] poured out,*" Yeshua, Jesus, Beloved Lord!

Chapter 28

# Her Signature Fragrance

**Song of Songs 6:9**

> *My dove, my perfect one, is the only one, the only one*
> *of her mother, the favorite of the one who bore her.*

EACH HEART IS A specific fragrance of God's heart. It is one of the perfumes filling our fragrant heart, as His Beloved.

We each have our own unique design, our own personal song to sing, our own personal fragrance to wear, and our own designer wedding dress. It is in our life's trials and victories, our weaknesses and strengths that create our signature fragrance and our glorious wedding dress. We must say, "Yes" to the dress the Holy Spirit is crafting for each of us to wear.

I want my fragrance to change the atmosphere wherever I go. This comes from me waiting on God, to be full of His knowledge. I want to know what part of the knowledge of God I am. What is the signature fragrance that God has placed in me, to be diffused every place I go?

**Song of Songs 4:16**
> *Awake, north wind,*
> *and come south wind!*
> *Blow on my garden,*
> *that its fragrance may spread abroad.*
> *Let my lover come into his garden*
> *and taste its chosen fruits.*

This has occurred in my own life many times, to bring forth the spices.

In this verse, a *garden* represents the soul of the believer. This includes all that involves her personality, her mind, her emotions, and her will.

In this song we learn that this is not a public garden, but one that is locked up. The soul of the believer has become a place where the Lord God can walk and fellowship intimately with the desire of His heart.

We know from the Scriptures that wind represents the Spirit of God. The Bride is inviting the North wind, which, in the natural, is very cold, to blow. I am living in the north now, and it is below freezing even as I write this. The cold is exaggerated when the wind blows, and it penetrates deeply and produces a bitter, biting chill.

She also called, in contrast, for the south wind, which we all love, to blow. It is a warm, gentle, and very pleasant wind and one that we all freely welcome.

What do the north and the south winds represent? They are different circumstances appointed by God to develop the fragrance of the garden in us and cause its fragrance to flow out to the world around us.

We must ask the Lord to send any circumstances which will cause the release of His Kingdom and then invite Him to come and enjoy Himself as He lives within.

As I look around my own surroundings here in the winter, with snow piled high everywhere, all that seems to remain alive in this season are the evergreen trees, which represent God's life, His life in you and me.

Chapter 29

# Out of the Dumpster

ONE OF THE MOST powerful revelations concerning the Bride came to me one day in the late 1990s when I was accompanying my husband Roy to the computer store one day. He had to pick up something he had ordered, and he asked me to go along. Afterward, he said, we could go get some lunch. I hated going to that computer store because I knew nothing about computers and found the experience to be very boring.

Roy was just the opposite. He found computers fascinating, he understood them, and was always wanting to learn more. To me it was like visiting a foreign country and hearing people speak in another language. It was only the thought of a nice lunch with my husband afterward that convinced me to go along. Maybe Roy's visit in the store this time would be short and sweet. At least that was my private hope.

He parked behind the store, which was located in a small strip mall, so that he could easily load whatever it was he had ordered, and, when he said he wouldn't be long, I decided just to wait in the car. It was wintertime, so I asked him to leave the engine running and the heater going.

There was no one else in sight, but as I waited for Roy to come back out, I saw an old man walking slowly down an alleyway. He was dirty and dressed poorly, like a homeless person. He would stop and look into the big green trash dumpsters behind the stores. I watched him for a while, and then he left. I never saw him find anything in those dumpsters.

I was sitting there thinking about this man when I heard the Holy Spirit saying to me, "Go look in that nearest dumpster."

My first thought was, "Now why would He want me to do that?" But when those words came to me again, and I felt an anointing coming upon me at the same time, I decided to obey.

I turned off the engine, got out of the car, and walked to the nearest green dumpster. The lid was closed. Still, I heard Him say, "Look inside."

I tried to lift the lid, but it was heavy. I began working at it, all the while thinking, "What if Roy comes out now and sees me doing this? What will I say?"

Finally, after many tries, I was able to open the lid enough to peer inside. It was very dark in there. I heard, "Get in."

This seemed beyond ridiculous, but I was able to climb up onto the top of the dumpster, and from there I could see better, and what I saw amazed me. There, deep inside the dumpster, were many beautifully wrapped bouquets of flowers. For some unknown reason, a flower shop had dumped them.

On top of the whole heap of flowers was a gorgeous bouquet of dozens of yellow roses — my favorites. They were in perfect condition, as if someone had just delivered them to my front door.

These flowers had not been cast off because they were wilted or brown around the edges. They seemed to be perfect in every way. What a shock to think that someone would just throw away perfectly good roses. Since no one else wanted them, and they were my favorites, I immediately decided to keep them. The Holy Spirit obviously wanted to bless me with these flowers and had shown me that they were inside that particular dumpster.

Was it really a trash dumpster? I looked again, and, yes, it was a trash dumpster, and there was trash under the flowers. I had not been wrong.

Then again, I heard the Holy Spirit saying, "Get inside and take a closer look." There was no one is sight, so I obeyed the Holy Spirit and climbed into the dumpster with the trash.

The trash was up to my knees, but I began moving it aside in an attempt to discover why I had been led to look further. I was amazed to discover more and more bouquets of lovely flowers, all professionally wrapped to protect them, and they were of many different colors. It was like finding a hidden treasure.

Roses were a treasure to me, and there were hundreds of them — yellow, red, pink, white, purple, and mixed hues. It was all so beautiful that I began to laugh and cry at the same time. Who could have discarded these gorgeous flowers to be dumped in a landfill and mixed with the real trash? I began picking out the best bouquets until my arms were overflowing with them.

I was able to climb my way out of the dumpster and jump to the ground, all the while looking around to see if anyone, including my husband, had come out and could see me getting out of the trash. There was no one.

I ran to the car, popped open the trunk, and began laying the dozens of roses I had loaded in my arms inside the trunk. I was laughing with joy at my great discovery as I brushed myself off and got back into the car.

Then the Holy Spirit spoke to me again, "Go back and get as many as you want."

I thought, "Well, why not? Why settle for a few dozen roses, when there were hundreds more there for the taking?"

I ran back and forth as fast as I could, climbing back into the dumpster, filling up my arms, and then climbing out again. I tried throwing some of the bouquets to the ground as carefully as I could, making sure not to damage any of them, and I kept filling the large trunk with beautiful flowers.

The roses had been on top, but under them were lilies and gladiolus, along with a few dozen carnations, red and white, and lots of extra greenery.

After several trips in and out of the dumpster, the trunk was packed. By this time, I was getting deeper and deeper into the dumpster, and each time my trip in and out was more difficult.

I was so full of the Holy Spirit while doing all of this that I cried, laughed, and got drunk with His joy and delight. When I found the gladiolus, all I could think of was a song we sang at that time that said, *He hath made me glad.* My words were now a little different: *He hath made me gladiolus. I will rejoice for He hath made me gladiolus.* I was singing that when space ran out. I closed the trunk and got back into the car to wait for Roy.

When he finally came out, he said the store had not received the computer items he needed after all, so he would have to return. It was a good thing because there was no room in the trunk for anything else.

He couldn't help but notice that the car was filled with wonderful fragrance. I told him I had found some discarded flowers and would like to get them home as quickly as possible before they wilted, but I didn't say how many there were. He agreed for us to go home and put the flowers in the refrigerator before going to lunch.

Unfortunately I wasn't able to see the expression on Roy's face when we got home and he popped the trunk open and looked inside. I can say that he was astonished at the quantity and quality of all the flowers I had collected.

The two of us began taking them inside, and they soon filled up the kitchen counters, the sink, and the tables. They were everywhere, and I had to do some explaining about where I had gotten so many flowers. Finally, when they were all inside, we decided to count them. To our amazement, there were 362 wrapped bouquets.

We began to wonder what we were supposed to do with so many flowers. We got out every vase we had and filled them with flowers, then every possible container of other types, but we ran out and needed so many more. I ran next door to ask my neighbor if she had any vases I could borrow and then gave her a bouquet of roses in her choice of colors.

I asked other neighbors if they had extra vases or containers I could borrow. I felt like the woman who was asked to fill the jars with oil and to go and find as many jars as she could and to keep pouring until she ran out of them (see 2 Kings 4:3-6). The fun part for me was inviting each neighbor to choose the flower bouquet they wanted. If they knew of someone who needed cheering up, we gave them an extra bouquet.

Some had special occasions coming up: "Oh, our anniversary is next week" or "My daughter's birthday is in a few days" or someone was coming home from the hospital with a new baby. We were able to provide flowers for them all. In the process of picking out the bouquet of flowers suited for each special occasion, we all laughed and rejoiced together. Such joy! Such love! It suddenly hit Roy and me that this was perhaps the very reason the Holy Spirit had showed me the hidden treasures of flowers, to share them with our neighbors and with other people needing encouragement. What a blessing they were!

In the coming days, I went to every hospital nearby, to the maternity wards, and the intensive care units, to retirement homes, funeral homes and to follow up on any leads that had come in by word of mouth, through phone calls or through the churches or our friends. You name it and I delivered flowers to them (some came by and picked them up at our home). It all reminded me of this psalm:

**Psalm 46:4 (AMP)**

*There is a river whose streams shall make glad the city of God [Yahweh].*

A River of Life now flowing out of me was making me glad (gladiolus), the City of God.

I kept asking the Lord over the following weeks if there was anything else He wanted me to know about the surprise treasure hunt. One obvious thought that came was that the Lord is taking His children out of the dumpsters, where others have discarded them. They saw little or no value in them, but He is putting them into beautiful vases or containers and placing them on display for others to see their beauty and worth. These are vessels of the Lord. Hallelujah!

Beloved, get ready to be surprised. Suddenly His hand might come down and pull you out of a terrible situation full of trash, and you will be surprised to find that the time in the dumpster has not affected your bouquet, or its fragrance. The character of your flowers is still the same. They are in perfect condition, for the Lord has protected and preserved you, and now it's your time to be seen, your time to be His scent, your time to be appreciated, your time to be valued, your time to be loved.

As the wise King Solomon said:

**Ecclesiastes 3:1**
*There is a time for everything,
    and a season for every activity under heaven.*

He makes everything beautiful in its time.

The Lord has embraced you in the shelter of His loving arms all along.

This was my time to learn that the Bride is made up of the people found in the gutters and the ghettos. Like the roses out of the dumpster, the Bride is made up of the unwanted, the abused, the outcasts, the discarded, the neglected, the torn, and the abandoned. This Bride, like the Shulamite maiden in the Song of Songs, sees herself as just ordinary, nothing special, and yet God promises:

**Isaiah 60:21**
*Then will all your people be righteous
    and they will possess the land forever.*

> *They are the shoot I have planted,*
> *the work of my hands,*
> *for the display of my splendor.*

**Isaiah 61:3**

> *... to bestow on them a crown of beauty*
> *instead of ashes,*
> *the oil of gladness*
> *instead of mourning,*
> *and a garment of praise*
> *instead of a spirit of despair.*
> *They will be called oaks of righteousness,*
> *a planting of the LORD*
> *for the display of his splendor.*

**1 Samuel 2:8 (AMP)**

> *He raises up the poor out of the dust and lifts up the*
> *needy from the ash heap, to make them sit with the*
> *noble and inherit the throne of glory.*

Clearly our God is up to something good.

Chapter 30

# The Bride Makes Herself Ready

PICTURE A WOMAN SITTING at her dressing table:

She is wearing her bridal gown.
The gown is magnificent, perfectly tailored to
fit her,
Chosen to display her bridal glory!

Her hair is perfect, clean, glistening.
Her skin is radiant.
She is glowing, brilliant.
She is seated at a dressing table looking into the
mirror,
When she hears the orchestra begin to play.
The wedding song has begun.

Her fragrance is intoxicating.
She is wearing her beloved Bridegroom's favorite scent.
She is anointed with royal oils and perfumes.
She makes one final glance into the mirror, making final adjustments.
Look down at her feet.
Her shoes are lovely, adorned with rose petals.

One last gesture is needed.
The music is beginning to crescendo.
Her heart is, too, beating fully, faster.
She feels it will burst open at any moment with pure joy.
Slowly and carefully she opens her treasure chest,
Where she keeps her precious jewels.
Reaching into the chest, she removes a string of stunning pearls.
"This is the final touch," she says, then, "I will be wed."
She can't believe it will be today.
She has waited her whole life.

She gently places the pearl necklace around her bare neck,
And as she is fastening it, the string breaks.
Gone … scattered … undone … the pearls disperse everywhere.

## The Bride Makes Herself Ready

Her heart drops, as does her face, into her hands.
She begins to weep.
They are all broken.
"My pearls are lost," she feels.

As she is weeping, the door opens into her bridal chambers.
She tries to look up, to see who it is.
Through her heavy, hot, tears she sees a figure.
It is one of her sons, watching her, hearing her cries.

He immediately comes to her side and kneels down at her feet.
She tries her best to tell him what has happened.
Between her sobs, he begins to get understanding.
She, the bride, is undone at the thought of losing her pearls.
Suddenly, but gently, the son begins to encourage her.
"See," he says, "I will get on my hands and knees
To help you recover all that was broken and appears lost.
We will find them all.
Not one pearl will be lost."
Because of the confident tone and love in his voice, her heart begins to lift.

"Yes, yes," she agrees, "let us look together and find them."

She wipes the tears away from her eyes and begins to look around.

Her son now is on his knees searching everywhere,
Under the bed, under the table, across the room.

She also is finding some that fell down into the folds of her dress.

Joy begins to build again in both of them.

"Here is one!" the son shouts, "Another one! Oh!"

Yes, they are now both shouting with joy, and saying, "We will recover them all.

None will be lost!"

The search continues with much excitement.

One by one, the pearls are rescued until …

She counts them. "All are here!" she cries.

The son picks up a golden thread and begins to string the pearls onto it.

"This gold is the strongest thread. It will not break again," he says.

Together they place each glistening translucent white pearl onto the golden thread.

Then the son adorns her neck, placing the pearl necklace for all to see.

Now, "See!" They both are in glee.

Nothing has been lost.

What was scattered has been gathered,
Pearls of great price redeemed.
She stands up.
The Bride has made herself ready with the sons of the
Kingdom's love.
Love never fails.

Now the music is deafening.
Worship is at its highest degree.
All eyes are on the door she is opening,
For all has been made ready.
Here comes His Bride!

This picture was given to me by Bob, one of my spiritual sons. I had asked him to write some comments regarding this book and his relationship with the Bride of Christ. One scripture that kept repeating itself in my spirit over and over while writing down this word picture was John 6:39-40, which states:

> *And this is the will of him who sent me, that I shall lose none of all that he has given me, but raise them up at the last day. For my Father's will is that everyone who looks to the Son and believes in him shall have eternal life, and I will raise him up at the last day.*

The purpose of including this picture of the Bride preparing herself according to Revelation 19:7, is that I believe it is a prophetic picture.

Jesus said:

**Matthew 19:12 (AMP)**

> *For there are eunuchs who have been born incapable of*
> *marriage; and there are eunuchs who have been made*
> *so by men; and there are eunuchs who have made them-*
> *selves incapable of marriage for the sake of the kingdom*
> *of heaven. Let him who is able to accept this accept it.*

In other words, there are special sons, spiritual eunuchs, who are part of the end-time company of Kingdom leadership who will not take the affections or attention of the Bride away from her beloved Bridegroom, Yeshua. They are called a *"friend"* (John 3:29, KJV). I strongly believe that only these spiritual eunuchs will be allowed to help the Bride recover any lost or broken pearls of promises, wisdom, or revelation. They have made themselves unable to reproduce anything but the Kingdom for the King of Glory.

These spiritual sons will always point her toward Him and not themselves or their ministry. They guard her heart, always knowing she belongs only to Him.

In great part, what I see the pearls on her necklace and wedding dress speak of are the pearls of wisdom and revelation of being called and chosen, remaining steadfast in the forming and the refining fire.

Chapter 31

# Who Is She?

**Song of Songs 3:6 (KJV)**

> *Who is this that cometh out of the wilderness like pillars of smoke, perfumed with myrrh and frankincense, with all powders of the merchant?*

**Song of Songs 6:10 (KJV)**

> *Who is she that looketh forth as the morning, fair as the moon, clear as the sun, terrible as an army with banners?*

WHO IS THIS RADIANT bride? She has the look and gaze of incandescence, as one who has been shut up in the eternal flames of Jesus' love:

**Song of Songs 8:5-6 (KJV)**

> *Who is this that cometh up from the wilderness, leaning upon her beloved? ... Set me as a seal upon thine*

*heart, ... the coals thereof are coals of fire, which hath
a most vehement flame.*

Who is she who ravishes the heart of the Father? Who is it who dwells safe and securely, sheltered in His shadow, there under His wings, there in the place where travail and threshing have been her portion. Who is it who has lifted her voice toward the heavens until she heard the echoing resound of His voice, that voice like unto the Honey in the Rock, who has been surrounded as it were by the Mahanaim or the two camps, His sent hosts of Heaven, who now stroll in His spice garden, partaking of the smell of kings' garments (aloes, cassia, and myrrh)?

Who? She is the Lamb's Wife, she who is arrayed, adorned, and crowned with His glory. Those who look to Him are radiant.

Not only is she presented to the Bridegroom as one who is radiant, but she is transparent, translucent, spotless, blameless, and ravished by His heart of love.

This Bride is forever surrounded by His eternal flames of glory. She is bejeweled, and she is crowned the Lamb's Wife.

Who, may we ask, is the Lamb's Wife? How do we know her? She is one who walks in and pursues intimacy with Him above all else. She is a passionate seeker of the Bridegroom's heart, for it is in His bosom that she finds her eternal place of refuge.

In his revelation, John heard these words:

**Revelation 19:7**

> *Let us rejoice and be glad and give him glory!*
> *For the wedding of the Lamb has come, and his bride*
> *has made herself ready.*

**Revelation 21:9**

> *One of the seven angels who had the seven bowls full*
> *of the seven last plagues came and said to me, "Come,*
> *and I will show you the bride, the wife of the Lamb."*

It is clearly God's will to reveal Jesus' Bride in the days ahead.

Chapter 32

# *Meeting Jesus in the Chuppah*

THROUGH THE YEARS, I began to see beautiful revelations for us, the Bride of Christ, through various Jewish wedding traditions. One of those is the *chuppah* or marriage canopy.

A *chuppah* is a canopy which sits atop four poles and is usually ornately decorated. The Jewish wedding takes place beneath this canopy, which is open on all sides. This is a demonstration of the couple's commitment to establish a home which will always be open to guests, just as was the tent of Abraham and Sarah.

Many Jewish couples actually erect the *chuppah* beneath the open skies. This recalls God's blessing to Abraham and his descendants to be as numerous as the stars. Furthermore, a *chuppah* under the open heavens symbolizes the couple's resolve to establish a household which will be dominated by heavenly and spiritual ideals.

## Meeting Jesus in the Chuppah

In preparation for the *chuppah*, the bride and groom untie any knots in their clothing, such as shoelaces, neckties, or bows. Nothing must impede them.

The *chuppah* itself can vary, but it is essentially a covered area where the bride and groom meet for the purpose of finalizing their nuptials. It is considered to be the groom's domain, and the bride consensually joining him beneath the roof is the symbolically unifying act which finalizes the marriage.

In modern-day Jewish betrothal ceremonies, the cloth for the *chuppah* is often a *tallit,* a Jewish prayer shawl. In some ceremonies the *tallit* is draped over the couple to indicate that the man will assume the protection and provision for his future wife. In our betrothal to Christ Jesus, we can be sure that He will protect us as part of His family.

Before the ceremony, the groom is led to a private room where he prepares himself for the *chuppah*. At this point, he removes any jewelry he may be wearing and empties his pockets of money or valuables. The bride, too, does not carry any money or valuables into the *chuppah*. The reason for this is that the bride and groom are committing to marry each other for who they are, not for what they may possess. This is symbolic that they will rely only on each other and what the Lord will provide for them as a couple, His blessings on them together. These are all beautiful symbols that prepare us to experience the *chuppah* with our Bridegroom Yeshua. Here comes the Bride and here comes the Groom too!

Chapter 33

# *The Beauty of the Mikvah*

**Luke 12:35-37**

> *Be dressed ready for service, and keep your lamps burning, like men waiting for their master to return from a wedding banquet, so that when he comes and knocks they can immediately open the door for him. It will be good for those servants whose master finds them watching when he comes. I tell you the truth, he will dress himself to serve, will have them recline at the table and will come and wait on them.*

IMAGINE IT! JESUS WILL gird Himself to serve us, like a waiter, laying aside His royal robes. He loves us so much, and He honors us so much that He serves us, when, actually, the wedding feast is in *His* honor.

Some preparation and planning is clearly indicated on the part of the Bride, and this is necessary to get her ready for what is to come. She has long been hidden, but now is about to emerge.

## The Beauty of the Mikvah

It was enlightening for me to discover what Jewish brides and grooms do to prepare themselves before the actual wedding. An important part of their preparation is called a *mikvah*, and the closer we can stay to Jewish tradition, while allowing all to be orchestrated by the Holy Spirit, the better.

MyJewishLearning.com states: "The *mikvah* or ritual bath signifies the spiritual rebirth of the bride and groom as they ponder their approaching marriage. The bride and groom's *mikvah* is a physical enactment of the passage from being unmarried to married. Entering the *chuppah* (marriage canopy) is a public declaration of a change in status. Entering the *mikvah* is a private transforming moment. It is a very satisfying experience — spiritually, emotionally, and aesthetically — when it is done honorably." [6]

I believe the key here is to ponder or meditate on the approaching life change through marriage. Traditionally the *mikvah* is a marking for the woman of an entrance into a new stage of her life. Since a *mikvah* involves bathing, many believe that it is a bathing away of impurities, but it is much more than that. It is not really about uncleanness, but about human encounters with the powers of the holy.

A *mikvah* can be done in any body of water that is living, as opposed to stagnant. It must be fresh and flowing. You may immerse two or three times, since this is the number of times the *mikvah* is mentioned in the *Torah*.

There are a number of Hebrew blessings that can be recited after rising from the immersion. One of those prayers is:

"Blessed are You, Lord Our God, Ruler of the Universe, who kept us alive and preserved us and enabled us to reach this season."

My favorite prayer recited at *mikvah* is the *Yehi Ratzon,* a prayer for the restoration of the Temple, a prayer envisioning a world as whole and pure as we hope to be upon emerging from our own personal *mikvah.*

Since it is a symbolic act, some choose to give the *mikvah* little value for today. However I discovered an interesting note in my studies on the subject, especially at MyJewishLe-arning.com and Chabad.org, that traditionally the Jewish people have come to give the *mikvah* such importance, that when building a new synagogue, they excavate the *mikvah* pool first, even before the main sanctuary. That says a lot.

Submitting to a *mikvah* has now become more of a joyful celebration or party, as it has inspired new rituals and celebrations among the younger generations. I rejoice with them, in their fresh revelation, as in Psalm 36:9:

**Psalm 36:9**

*For with you is the fountain of life;*
*in your light we see light.*

Part IV

# The Emerging
# Bride Gathering

Chapter 34

# A Vision That Changed My Life

**Acts 16:9-10**

*During the night Paul had a vision of a man of Macedonia standing and begging him, "Come over to Macedonia and help us." After Paul had seen the vision, we got ready at once to leave for Macedonia, concluding that God [Yahweh] had called us to preach the gospel to them.*

**Romans 10:15**

*How can they preach unless they are sent? As it is written, "How beautiful are the feet of those who bring good news!"*

THIS FIRST PASSAGE, FROM Acts, reveals that Paul was given a vision, one of the ways the Holy Spirit speaks to us still. I, too, was given a vision regarding being asked to come over to Ontario, Canada, to help the Canadian people understand the bridal revelation. This also included being sent to preach and prophesy to those asking for help.

This call to *"come over"* had been in my spirit for a long time. In 1988, while still living in Kansas City, we were attending a Charismatic church, and a guest minister, an apostle, came there from Canada to speak. The night before seeing this man I was given a prophetic word for him. I was remembering it when I woke up the next day and as we left for the church service.

The man, in his eighties, was very humble and anointed. After he had finished ministering to all the people, I went over to give him the prophetic word the Lord had given me during the night. As I drew near to him, there was so much glory coming from him that I could hardly stand in his presence.

He was one of the most humble people I have ever met, and like a father, he reached out to me and said, "Go ahead, and give me the word." I hadn't said anything to him yet, but he knew by the Spirit that I had a word for him. Doubled over, I prophesied to him.

Only one portion of what was said that day remained in my heart. The rest I cannot remember. The part I did remember was that the Lord was going to begin to send apostles and prophets from Canada to the United States and from the United States into Canada. As I said this, I had a vision of a sewing machine stitching back and forth along the borders between the two nations. I discovered that the word meaning *to stitch* in Hebrew also means "to mend or heal." I heard the Holy Spirit say to this man, "These two nations have been neighbors, but I want them to become sisters and brothers."

The brother thanked me and affirmed that this was exactly why he had come to the U.S. and that he would hide this word in his heart and cherish it.

I wasn't sure why someone like me, then living in the heart, or center, of the U.S., had been given a word like this, but since the Holy Spirit had quickened it to me, like Mary, the mother of Jesus, I held it in my heart in the days ahead.

Chapter 35

# Our Move To Upstate New York

AFTER WE HAD BEEN living in Kansas City for thirty-one years, the Holy Spirit spoke to me one day very clearly and said, "You are moving to Upstate New York where your husband is from. Go and tell him right now."

Roy had long wanted to move back to his roots along the St. Lawrence River in New York. We had visited there many times over the years, but I loved where we were and did not like what I considered to be the depressed nature of that area of New York. So, every time he had brought it up through the years, I had always answered him, "No way!" (Believe me, I have a purpose in telling this part of the story. I wish to testify to the faithfulness of the Lord to watch over His word to perform it, regardless of whether or not we personally want it.)

## Our Move To Upstate New York

One day, while I was walking across the room, the Holy Spirit spoke these words very clearly to me and told me to go find Roy and tell him, "You are moving to Upstate New York. I decided to obey, thinking that it would surely be a very long time before what the Lord was saying would really happen.

I found Roy and told him, "We are moving to Upstate New York," and his eyes began to tear up. He said, "Well, that has to be God, because I know you don't like it up there and have never wanted to move there." I didn't encourage him further. I just told him what God had said.

To my way of thinking, that was it. Okay, I had been obedient, and now I was ready to forget the whole thing and move on.

But I was in for a big surprise. It was almost a blur how fast things began to fall into place. Like a snowball going downhill, this idea took on its own momentum, and Roy was suddenly ready to move. I had told him what God had said, but was I really ready for this thing to actually happen and so soon?

Several things happened to ease our way: (1) Our adult children decided to come with us — our daughter and her husband and children to settle there, and our adult son Adam to help us move and get settled, and (2) Jobs opened up that summer for extra income for the moving trucks. The thought of having grandchildren come along made the idea of the move a little easier for me ... a little.

Soon after I had spoken of it for the first time, some of the family got online and began looking for a house big enough for all of us to share. Not me, of course. I wanted it all to either fail or to move very slowly. To the contrary, I could see that it was quickly taking on a life of its own, and everyone else but me was happy about the idea.

To make a long story short, we did find a suitable house. It was located a few miles from Roy's family on the river overlooking Canada. There was a huge picture window in the living room looking straight out over the St. Lawrence to Ontario on the other shore. I was sure that was not a mistake. There is no Hebrew word for *coincidence*. I needed to get myself ready to move.

Chapter 36

# *Getting Started in this New Ministry*

AFTER WE HAD MOVED to New York, for the first few years the Holy Spirit kept reminding me of that prophecy I had given to the apostle from Canada. I was now living on the border of those two nations, just minutes from the bridge that connected them.

We began attending a nearby church, and the first lady I met turned out to be from the Canada side. She and her husband had been coming over for years. What a divine set-up that was!

They invited us to a tent meeting, and we decided to go. When we arrived, we saw two rows of chairs set out with an open aisle down the center between them. Roy and I went to a front-row seat and began to worship.

As I was worshipping I had a clear vision of a Canadian flag coming down and being draped over our shoulders. I received a scripture from Genesis that said something about no longer being strangers or aliens to these people. I was weeping because of the glory I felt in that vision.

After it faded, the worship leader asked, "Who is from Canada?" and then "Who is from the states?" As God is my witness, everyone on the side where we were seated raised their hands with the first question. They were all from Canada. There were Americans present, but they were all sitting on the other side.

It was unbelievable, like a Red Sea event for us. The Holy Spirit had done the parting of the waters of people, and we were found counted with the Canadians, just as I had seen in the vision.

The Lord now had my undivided attention, and I was contemplating all of this on our way back home that night. In my heart, I still wanted to go back to Kansas City. That was somehow still "home" for me. God had other ideas.

We attended that tent meeting one other night. A woman from out of state was ministering prophetically. She came down the aisle and asked if a lady from Canada was my friend. We had just met, so we said no, not really, but under that anointing she began to prophesy that the Canadian lady and I would become "sisters in the Lord." They were the same words the Holy Spirit had used in 1988.

I was so undone by all that the Holy Spirit was speaking to us that I was on the ground in the sawdust. What must we do? I asked the Lord about this, and He reminded me of more of the prophecy I had given the apostle from Canada, He said, "Now you are a part of helping this come to pass."

I now entered into a serious time of seeking the Lord's face and waiting on Him, to learn what He wanted me to do. Lying there on the floor, I had a vision of a scepter being extended to me from Jesus' hand. He told me He was giving me His authority to go into Canada as one of the apostles and prophets to connect His people there to His plans and purposes. My entire commission regarded showing them the Bride-Bridegroom revelation and calling them to know Him in this glorious dimension. He told me He wanted to see His reflection on their faces and not "a northern one." I later learned, after living here in New York for a while, that there was a favorite store in both the U.S. and Canada called Northern Reflections. It was very popular, so when God said it that way, He was speaking their language.

Now, like Queen Esther, I was released to go over to the Canadians *"for such a time as this"* (Esther 4:14). There was more to the vision, but this is sufficient for now.

Chapter 37

# The Dorcas Anointing

I WANT TO EXPLAIN ANOTHER vital part to the prophecy about the Macedonian call to Canada. The vision of the sewing machine stitching together the two nations, as told to me by the Holy Spirit, was like a Dorcas anointing. My entire life I had never known anyone by that name. I was now living in New York and been told to go over to Ontario, Canada, to help people with the bridal paradigm.

Through a series of phone calls and inquiring, I found a place nearby that I had seen in another vision. This vision was of two long harvest tables, as I called them, in a farm-house. Where in the world might that be? As I was talking to the women's leader in the church we were attending, she said, "Don't you remember? We had a women's retreat there."

I reminded her that I had been unable to attend that particular retreat, so she gave me directions to the place, and off I went, a few days later, to find that farmhouse. Within fourteen minutes, I had located it and was looking through the window at the very harvest tables I had seen in my vision. Oh, I was so excited!

I called the lady back and asked her how I could reach the owners of this place? She gave me a phone number but said that it was long distance. The woman lived in Pennsylvania.

"What?" I said. "They don't even live here in New York?"

"No," I was told.

I called the lady excitedly, and I'm afraid I was talking so fast it was hard for her to grasp what I was trying to say. When I finished, I asked what her name was. "Dorcas," she said. With that, I think I may have screamed into the phone. Dorcas hung in there and didn't hang up on me. Needless to say, it was a divine appointment and a confirmation to the prophetic word I was given about the two nations and the Dorcas anointing. Glory to His name! He is Faithful and True!

Dorcas explained to me that she and her husband had felt the urging of the Holy Spirit to buy that farm in New York and remodel it to be used for special events. Their prayer was that it would be for the salvation of many souls. What a beautiful farm! And now it was being used for God's glory and purposes.

Dorcas said we could use it for gatherings or retreats or any other use we needed it for, even family reunions. I hadn't seen the entire inside yet, but I had a witness that Dorcas and I would meet soon and become close sisters in God's Kingdom.

Chapter 38

# The Genesis of the Bridal Gathering

I RECEIVED A PROPHETIC word saying that I would soon be emerging into my true calling, and not long after that I miraculously found my new sister Gloria Reid online in Virginia. I had found her by searching for "new oils" and, of course, it was a Holy Spirit set-up.

At first, Gloria and I connected only by phone, but somehow we knew immediately that we were to plan something together. Over the weeks that followed we e-mailed each other dozens of times, and we could see that we had more in common than we first realized.

Gloria sent me sample bottles of the oils from her new series called the Emerging Bride. We shared a common language as well as many common desires.

Gloria had been planning to go to Israel that spring to pour out the new oils there first, but as we talked more,

## The Genesis of the Bridal Gathering

I asked her if she would ever consider coming to Upstate New York to spend time with me and a group of women who loved the Lord. They wanted to learn more about the oils and teachings on the Jewish wedding traditions. She agreed, saying we could tag-team with the teaching, she with teachings on the oils, and me with teachings on the Jewish wedding events.

In preparation, Gloria sent me sixteen large bottles (not just sample size) of the Emerging Bride oils, so that I could not only smell them, but could begin to wear them and intercede with each one, to receive the understanding and the impartation from each.

The ladies I had in mind, when I invited Gloria to come to New York, were a group of close-knit friends, sisters in the Lord, who had a similar vision. In fact, some of us had banded together to form a ministry known as Key Ministries, and we were working together.

Margriet Hintz from Brockville, Ontario, Canada, was prominent among that group, and we also had a large group from Pennsylvania. All of us prayed about who else to invite. Friends, new and old, were added one by one to the list as the Holy Spirit revealed them to us. Those who were invited were from Canada, New York, and Pennsylvania, but also from California, Missouri, and Michigan. So they would be coming from the north, the south, the east, and the west. The Holy Spirit called each of them, and they answered. In this way, it happened that the new line of Emerging Bride

## Threads of Gold

oils were poured out in Ogdensburg, New York, a very small town no one had heard of, instead of in Jerusalem, and an event took place that turned our lives upside down.

Chapter 39

# Planning and Preparation

MUCH PLANNING WENT INTO this event, as with a real wedding. It took months to prepare. Gloria began to mail ahead the boxes of oils and other gifts she would need when she was teaching. Together we prayed about not only who to invite, but also where to meet, for how many days, and the specific dates.

A number of the women who wanted to attend had jobs and needed to ask for time off. This gathering was to be multi-generational, as young and old alike were invited. Even a couple of uninvited people showed up, led by the Lord in His perfect timing.

Our sister Dorcas agreed that we could rent the farmhouse for this occasion so that everyone could be together. The farm sleeps sixteen. She is a beautiful sister with a heart of gold and a gift of hospitality. God had given her and her husband the farmhouse to share with the community for a reason. She is great at organizing meals, and all of us pitched in for the food.

Meanwhile, Margriet, Gloria, and I were pressing into the Lord to see what He wanted to do when we got together and what special provisions we needed to buy. He had me buy special perfume bottles. They were hand-blown and of all different shapes and colors, representing each bride (or lady) coming.

The Lord sent Margriet on a fantastic shopping spree to find special gifts to be placed on a table for each lady to choose the one she desired after she received ministry time in the *chuppah*. Margriet had so much fun going on this see-and-find shopping spree with the Holy Spirit and found amazing gifts to give to each sister. Everyone loved them!

Chapter 40

# A Surprise for Me

ONE DAY, WHILE I was writing this story, I got a box delivered to my front door. In it was a new pair of shoes. They were leather-woven moccasins in the color fuchsia, and the inside lining was in silver, with fuchsia and blue flowers on it. And they were just my size.

To make this even more exciting, it was snowing outside, huge fat white snowflakes reported to be about six to eight inches across. What hope those beautiful spring-colored moccasins brought to me on a snowy and bitter-cold winter's day!

You may be wondering what all of this has to do with the message of the emerging Bride. Well, an important part of who I am was beginning to emerge, and the colors were significant.

Colors have always been important to me because they're important to my Father. He made the colors, and the shoes were fuchsia and pink. Fuchsia stands for passion, joy, right relationships, compassion, a heart of flesh, a passion for Yeshua (Jesus), the Bridegroom's heart, *koinonia* (fellowship), a deep place of the heart.

Pink is for Messiah, the Rose of Sharon, the Father's heavenly care, the lilies of the field, His children (Jesus loves me! This I know.), right relationships, romance, compassion, and compassion for Jesus.

The silver inside the shoes was for redemption, the Word of God, freedom, strength, atonement, freedom to create, divinity, righteousness, strengthened faith, wisdom, and purity.

The baby blue of the flowers was for heavenly, bride, divinity, seated with the Lord in heavenly places, the Holy Spirit, grace, healing, an open heaven, and overcomer.

The bottoms of the shoes were raised butterflies.

A new pair of shoes, according to Ira Milligan's dream interpretation book, [7] signifies a new ministry or way of life. I know this wasn't a dream I had, but I believe this interpretation can still apply somewhat, as the Holy Spirit directs.

Shoes have to do with the Gospel covenant preparation. In Ephesians 6:15, the word *feet* can also mean "heart" and your feet (heart) shod with the Gospel of peace. *Feet* here speak of heart-walk, way, thoughts.

**Galatians 5:16**

> *So I say, live [walk, KJV] by the Spirit, and you will not gratify the desires of the sinful nature [the lusts of the flesh, KJV].*

By receiving these new shoes in a snowstorm, I was planning ahead to be prepared to have my heart (or feet) shod with the Gospel of peace.

The size of the shoes, seven, indicated completeness, perfection which only comes from walking in the Spirit, who is the Perfect One and completes us in Christ. Although I would never wear those particular shoes during the cold season, I would be prepared or made ready for the next season with the Lord.

This was the same process we used for the preparations for the Emerging Bride Gathering. Months ahead of time, all of the needed supplies were secured and shipped and stored at the appointed place of meeting. The Holy Spirit, during prayer, told us to actually purchase wedding invitations and send them out to those names we had been interceding over. It was His list of choices, not ours, of who to invite. He was preparing us for something wonderful.

**Song of Songs 2:10-13**

*Arise, my darling, my beautiful one,*
   *and come with me.*
*See! The the winter is past;*
   *the rains are over and gone.*
*Flowers appear on the earth;*
   *the season of singing has come,*
   *the cooing of doves is heard in our land.*

## Threads of Gold

*The fig tree forms its early fruit;*
*    the blossoming vines spread their fragrance.*
*Arise, come, my darling;*
*    my beautiful one, come with me.*

Those shoes blessed my soul.

Chapter 41

# *His Leading*

AS WE EXAMINED AND reexamined in prayer our motivations for the upcoming event, we were careful to allow the Spirit to lead us in each and every point,

We were led to call the gathering The Emerging Bride Gathering. To *emerge*, we found, meant "to move out of or away from something and come into view." We were not sure what we were moving toward, but it was exciting. We were led to have it in July (of 2010). As it turned out, it was hot enough for the first time ever to need to go out and buy air-conditioners for the windows downstairs.

Since bridal love is always voluntary, all of the daughters who were to attend the gathering had to be hand-picked by the Lord, and they each had to come voluntarily because of love for their Bridegroom-King and no other reason. Therefore it was not a large gathering. In all, there were sixteen of us who gathered at the farmhouse in Upstate New York.

The week before the other sisters arrived, two of my friends came for an early visit. Two of us were old friends, but we hadn't seen each other for years. I had just met Linda for the first time in person. All of us had been interceding on the phone together, along with all the other ladies. Dorcas allowed us to stay at the farmhouse those days too, so that we could catch up and also prepare the house for the gathering.

It was a glorious time together. We worshiped, danced, and cleaned the house spiritually, as well as ourselves. We wanted everything to be perfect for the coming days.

We had all the provisions for the *chuppah* coming with the group from Pennsylvania. Everything was falling into place.

Chapter 42

# My Friend Bob Comes By

ONE DAY BEFORE ALL the women would gather together, and I would finally meet Gloria face to face for the
first time, Bob, an old friend of mine, called and asked if he
could come and spend a day with us, praying and prophesying over us for the coming event. I was a little troubled about
this at first because I was so focused on what God was doing
with the ladies, but I soon got peace about it.

After Bob arrived, I saw that it was all tied together. His
ministry blessed us and him to have the time to re-connect
since it had been sixteen years since we last saw each other
(sixteen is the number of love). We laughed, cried, and
waited on the *Ruach*, and then Bob spoke to all of us.

The Holy Spirit had told him that he was going to trim
the wicks of five wise virgins, and they would be filled with
fresh oil. This happened through our prayer and worship.
The five women present were: Elaine, Mary Ellen Wright,
Linda Vaughan, Dorcas Breckbill, and Linda Kahler.

The next morning, at daylight, Bob left, and within hours all the other ladies arrived by car and plane. We were ecstatic — meeting new sisters for the first time but feeling like old friends. Only the Holy Spirit can accomplish that.

We settled in, finding our rooms and sleeping arrangements, eating good food, and then, coming together, we worshiped and waited.

Chapter 43

# *The Threshing Mats*

THAT FIRST NIGHT GLORIA gave me a threshing mat she had made for our ministry group then known as Key Ministries. It was beautiful. It had two keys on it crossed with white lace from an old wedding gown sown into it. The mat itself was made from burgundy red velvet material, and it was plush and rich looking, suitable for royalty. She had written us a note: "While working on your mat, He gave directions on all the embellishment and adornments."

- The twelve stars of David (Revelation 22:17) represent the eternal foundations of the New Jerusalem's tree [important to me since I am a Messianic Jew].
- The Holy Spirit, the Bridegroom, is represented by a man's tie.
- The Bride is represented by a piece from a woman's bridal gown.

- The two gold keys to unlock eternity are in the union of the Bridegroom and His Bride, made up of many tribes and tongues.
- The iridescent buttons represent all of the white light at God's throne, containing all the colors of the spectrum.
- Four is the number of bringing Heaven to Earth, and represents the sealed work of God.
- Sixteen scraps of bridal fabric were used because sixteen is the number of love (see John 3:16 and 1 John 4:16).

What did it all mean? The Lord had been speaking to a sister about a kneeling prayer rug. She was in the military in Iraq, and the Lord instructed her, as a Christian, to get a mat and begin to kneel on it in prayer and to intercede for that country. She sanctified the mat to the Lord God of Israel first, then began to pray on it. When she put it away, the Lord told her to get it out again and use it as a point of contact for our troops in Iraq and the people of that country.

The prayer rug or mat can be traced back to its ancient Hebrew roots. The word *rug* is derived from a word meaning "bed," because a rug was a portable bed for the nomadic people who traveled in the desert. They ate on it, slept on it, and rested on it.

In Hebrew, *kneeling* is the root word for *worship*. How often do we stop and kneel on a rug and pray? Other cul-

tures kneel before foreign gods. Why have we lost the custom
of kneeling to the living God?

The reason Gloria had produced these mats was because she
wanted to give the Lord God of Abraham, Isaac, and Jacob
(Israel) all glory as we knelt to pray. The Lord is restoring the
tabernacle of David (worship). He will restore these mats to His
people as a powerful point of contact. After much prayer, we
decided to call them the Threshing Floor Prayer Rugs (or mats).

Gideon met with the Angel of the Lord on the threshing
floor. Threshing is a means of harvesting. We want to harvest
souls, and the best place to start is on our knees. *The Dictionary of Biblical Imagery* [8] states that threshing was so much part
of the process of producing food in ancient times that, along
with the winepress, the threshing floor summed up harvest and
plowing and, therefore, God's provision for His people (see
Deuteronomy 16:13 and Joel 2:24).

We were on the threshold of the Lord's promises, and we
symbolically knelt on the threshing floor in front of the threshold of Heaven. I could see the validity in this for the point of
contact, for our troops especially.

The entire threshing mat carrier was embellished with
gold. After receiving this beautiful gift, all the women of
Key Ministries took a turn on the threshing mat interceding
and threshing with our sisters and mothers, with the Spirit's
help. It was a reverent and holy time together. We rejoiced
and laughed after sowing in tears, knowing that we would
bear much fruit from this time well spent.

Chapter 44

# Discerning the Meaning of the Mats

**Isaiah 66:7 (AMP)**

*Before [Zion] travailed, she gave birth; before her pain came upon her, she was delivered of a male child.*

**Micah 4:13**

*Arise and thresh,*
*O Daughter of Zion;*
*for I will give you horns of iron;*
*I will give you hoofs of bronze,*
*and you will break to pieces many nations.*

GLORIA HAD BROUGHT A threshing mat of her own, so we took turns on the two mats. We divided into two groups, and one-by-one we prayed for each sister as she was actually threshing/travailing. It was an act of trust for them to be transparent, vulnerable, and humble before total strangers with the help of the Holy Spirit. The emerging Bride was risen from the threshing floor.

The purpose of the act of threshing is to separate and divide certain elements one from another. The end result is always the same, to bring forth the chosen element to be established and then to have the remaining elements removed. There should be no mixture in the final element. It is to be pure.

When we are threshing, we are declaring those things that are not as though they were (see Romans 4:17). We are also decreeing that all those things which oppose the declaration be cast off, cast aside, torn, trodden down, trampled, and broken. The result is a separation of the pure from the profane.

*Thresh* and *threshing* relate to decision making, so we are deciding, declaring and dividing. *Decision* means "thresh."

One could say that the act of threshing represents a resolute decision to become firm about the status of a thing, to become immoveable and thresh (decide) past the Valley of Indecision on the matters we face. It is to call forth a decision, to push aside, clear away, or eradicate anything that stands opposing that which has been declared.

As each lady had her personal turn on the threshing mat, she was making an absolute decision to become firm about the status of being Christ's Bride and declaring, by that decision, to be divided (separated) from anything in opposition and for that opposing thing to be removed or cast off.

**Joel 3:14**

> *Multitudes, multitudes in the valley of decision!*

**Psalm 68:1 (KJV)**

> *Let God arise, let his enemies be scattered: let them also that hate him flee before him.*

In other words, let all those who oppose His eternal Words and purposes be separated, like chaff from the wheat, like darkness from light.

As Jesus taught us to pray:

**Matthew 6:10 (KJV)**

> *Thy kingdom come, Thy will be done in earth, as it is in heaven.*

What results is a pure Bride:

**Revelation 21:9**

> *Come, I will show you the bride, the wife of the Lamb.*

The Lamb's wife is adorned and crowned. By the end of the weekend the Lord would adorn His Bride, His Beloved, with His crown and scepter.

## Discerning the Meaning of the Mats

Those threshing times on the mats were vital to the intimacy we would all experience through repentance, confession, forgiveness, and being absolved of all sin. Then the Spirit and fruit of joy were released, after our cleansing time ended through the blood of Yeshua being applied through prayer, worship, and travail.

Chapter 45

# *The Mikvah*

I SHARED WITH THE women briefly about the traditional Jewish *mikvah* that night and told them that we would each later enjoy a personal *mikvah*.

Gloria had obtained individual bars of special soap for us to bathe with that first night (or early the next morning if they preferred) in preparation for the teaching on the betrothal in Jewish tradition the next day. The name of the soap was *Come Away My Beloved* and had fragrant oil of myrrh infused in it.

Since we, a group of women, were not about to go outside and immerse ourselves in a lake or the yet cold water of the St. Lawrence River, the Holy Spirit gave us a much simpler, yet just as effective, way. We would each meet with Him in the shower.

With Jewish couples, the *mikvah* is a prophetic act of faith, and it was with us as well. Therefore, we felt justified in adapting it to our particular circumstances.

At the end of the evening, we gave each lady one of the soaps for her very own private and personal *mikvah* with the Holy Spirit. They each took their *Come Away With Me* soap and went to prepare to meet alone with Him. This would prepare them for the next ministry event. We encouraged them to take their time and not hurry and to sing to the Lord a new song as they bathed. Each lady then went her way and performed her own Spirit-led *mikvah*.

Chapter 46

# The Anointing of a Queen/Bride

THE NEXT DAY GLORIA taught us on the Emerging Bride oils, their significance, and their preparation. She emphasized the high price of each oil and what it costs to wear it, reminding us all of her threshing and intercession, as she waited on the Lord to hear what essential oils were to go into each scent, how many drops of each element, their compatibility, and the essence derived from their combination. This is the Bride being the waiter, serving the King in this age.

Then we performed an ancient Hebrew custom, the anointing of a queen-bride. As every lady took her turn being brought forth, she received gifts of the scents (anointing oils) poured by Gloria, and she proceeded to anoint each emerging bride with the ten fragrant oils. This created a throne, like a mountain of spices, for the Bridegroom-King Yeshua to be enthroned upon, as in Song of Songs 8:14. He, Yeshua, received our commitments and worship. Anointed with covenant colors and holy scents, the Bride is His mountain of spices, and we see her desire for Him.

In Revelation 11, the Bride is crying out with all the redeemed:

**Revelation 11:15**
> *The kingdom of this world has become the kingdoms*
> *of our Lord and of his Christ,*
> *and he will reign for ever and ever.*

The King is coming!

The women had begun their preparations, like Queen Esther, on the threshing mat, to make their decision for His Kingship-Lordship. They had all come through the spiritual preparation of their *mikvah* of song and scents. Each had made her way slowly, at her own personal pace (with the help of the Holy Spirit), through this birth canal of sound (worship) and scent (anointing oils). We couldn't wait to see what came next.

Chapter 47

# The Scents Released

THE FOLLOWING IS A list of the twelve fragrant oils released to represent the Emerging Bride. Explanations and personal experiences are given with some of them. We are indebted to Gloria and her husband, who printed a scroll with the list of names for the Emerging Bride Oils:

1. Eternal Flame – (Song of Songs 8:6)
2. Radiant (Psalm 34:5)
3. Ravished Heart (Song of Songs 4:9)
4. My Portion (Psalm 16:5)
5. Spice Garden (Song of Songs 4:16)
6. Under His Wings (Psalm 91)
7. Two Camps (Song of Songs 6:13)
8. Travail (Isaiah 66:7)
9. Sheltered (Psalm 61:3)
10. Honey in the Rock (Psalm 81)

11. Lamb's Wife (Revelation 21:9)
12. King's Favor (Psalm 45)

More details came later, as Gloria provided more insight on the ingredients of the oils and their significance.

We all had a wonderful dinner, fellowshipped, and then went to bed. An excitement to experience a personal time in the *chuppah* was increasing in many of the ladies.

Chapter 48

# *Discerning the Meaning of the Oils*

## 1. ETERNAL FLAME

**Song of Songs 8:6 (KJV)**
*Set me as a seal upon thine heart, as a seal upon thine arm: for love is strong as death; jealousy is cruel as the grave: the coals thereof are coals of fire, which hath a most vehement flame.*

In other words, wear me as a seal close to your heart.

*Set* here means "to put with a design-exact fit for some special purpose."

*Seal* means "signet, or signature ring."

*Upon* means "principal of identification."

This *"most vehement flame"* of Jehovah is lightning. It is a blue flame of unquenchable love. This love is compared to the very fire of Yahweh. It is a vehement love, like unto the menorah flame that never goes out.

Paul wrote:

**2 Corinthians 11:2**

*I am jealous for you with a godly jealousy ... that I might present you as a pure virgin to him [Jesus].*

In Zechariah 1:14, the Lord says that His desire for Jerusalem and Zion makes Him exceedingly jealous for her. For those who would be bridal souls, the Lord has intolerable jealousy toward any false lovers. This includes any idols or things of the earth that might come between Him and His Bride. She must be purified with an eternal flame that will purge and make her as pure as gold. The Lord's jealousy is like flashes of fire, removing any spot or blemish.

†

# 2. RADIANT

**Psalm 34:5**

*Those who look to him are radiant;*
*their faces are never covered with shame.*

The reason is that they have a radiant heart of joy.

This psalm was sung to the four hundred who gathered with David in the cave of Adullam. They were those who had come out of the house of Saul and been separated from the old order and its table. This is an example of threshing, which, as we have seen, means to make a decision, to be separated. These mighty men laid their lives and reputations on the line in the wilderness of discipline to be a part of David's kingdom.

As we looked to our Bridegroom during this difficult time apart, we would become radiant. We were to look to Him expectantly and be lightened. *Lightened* means "brightened up." Our faces (hearts) were never to be ashamed. We should reflect like a glass mirror what we have looked upon. Therefore our countenance should look like Him.

One of the ingredients of this oil is *neroli*, which speaks of peace.

Who is this so radiant? She has the look and gaze of an incandescent Bride, as one who has been shut up in the eternal flames of His fire (see Song of Songs 5:5-6).

†

# 3. RAVISHED HEART

**Song of Songs 4:9**
> *You have stolen my heart , my sister, my bride;*
> *you have stolen my heart with one glance of your*
> *eyes, with one jewel of your necklace.*

**Song of Songs 4:9 (KJV)**

> *Thou hast ravished my heart, my sister my spouse;*
> *thou hast ravished my heart with one of thine eyes,*
> *with one chain of thy neck.*

Who is she that has ravished the heart of the Father?
*Ravished* means "to excite or inflame the heart." *"You have stolen my heart."*

In Song of Songs 4:8, the Lord addresses the maiden for the first time as "My Bride." Previously He had asked her to *"come away"* with Him. Now He is able to call her to *"come with Me,"* as they are now in union. Paul wrote:

**1 Corinthians 6:17 (AMP)**

> *The person who is united to the Lord becomes one*
> *spirit with him.*

The spirit of Yahweh becomes so co-mingled with the spirit of man that you can no longer separate the two. In fact, they are no longer two, but one.

Two things have been mentioned that ravish the King's heart. One is a single glance of her eye. The second is a single strand of her necklace. Jesus said:

**Luke 11:34-36**

> *Your eye is the lamp of your body. When your eyes*
> *are good, your whole body is full of light. But when*

*they are bad, your body also is full of darkness. See to it, then, that the light within you is not darkness. Therefore, if your whole body is full of light, and no part of it dark, it will be completely lighted, as when the light of a lamp shines on you.*

In other words, for those who have a single, or clear, eye, their whole body will be full of light.

*Eye* here means "insight." *Neck* means "will." The Bride holds close to her heart His covenant promises.

The Bride's eye is single, like that of a dove. She is separated unto Him, her risen and living King.

†

## 4. MY PORTION

**Psalm 16:5**

*Lord, you have assigned me my portion and my cup; you have made my lot secure.*

**Deuteronomy 32:9**

*For the Lord's portion is his people Jacob his allotted inheritance.*

With each anointing oil, there is a portion that is found in the chambers of intimacy with our Bridegroom, King Jesus. He is our portion. He is all we need, want, or desire.

## Discerning the Meaning of the Oils

This was given to my friend and sister Gloria through the beautiful and sacred hymn, and she stated it so beautifully and eloquently, as the refrain says:

> *In Jesus is my portion,*
> *My constant friend is He.*
> *His eye is on the sparrow*
> *And I know He watches me.* [9]

Because He is our portion, we can take all comfort in every situation concerning all things in this life. This reminds me of the Parable of the Ten Virgins in Matthew 25:1-13. It is a parable of the harvest, and Jesus is speaking about believers and compares the five wise virgins with the five foolish virgins. He is speaking of those who know Him and states that He is coming again for His Bride.

All the virgins had lamps (our lives and/or ministries). All the virgins' lamps were lit. They all had received Jesus as their personal Savior, were all born-again. What, then, made the difference in the virgins to be called either *"wise"* or *"foolish"*? Jesus said:

### Matthew 25:3

> *The foolish ones took their lamps but did not take any*
> *oil with them.*

Oil is symbolic of the Holy Spirit. Oil can also represent intimacy, our relationship, the oil of pure revelation. Only the wise had oil in their jars. In other words, they had their unique portion.

Again we read:

**Matthew 25:6**

*At midnight the cry rang out, "Here's the bridegroom. Come out to meet him!"*

Because the Bridegroom was a long time coming, they had all slumbered and fallen asleep. Upon hearing this cry, all the virgins woke up and trimmed their lamps.

**Matthew 25:8**

*The foolish ones said to the wise, "Give us some of your oil [your personal portion]; our lamps are going out."*

The wise virgins refused:

**Matthew 25:9**

*"No," they replied, "there may not be enough for both us and you. Instead, go to those who sell oil and buy some for yourselves [get your own special portion].*

The foolish virgins decided to do this, but it was too late:

## Discerning the Meaning of the Oils

**Matthew 25:10**

*But while they were on their way to buy the oil, the bridegroom arrived. The virgins who were ready went in with him to the wedding banquet. And the door was shut.*

The foolish virgins eventually got to the feast, but they were late:

**Matthew 25:11**

*Later the others also came. "Sir! Sir! they said, "Open the door for us!"*

The reply they received was startling:

**Matthew 25:12**

*But He replied, "I tell you the truth, I do not know you."*

At midnight (such as our world now finds itself in, with its moral and spiritual darkness) the coming of the Bridegroom, our Lord, was announced. The virgins trimmed their lamps. This word *trimmed* in the original Greek, means "to put in proper order." All their lamps had been lit before they slumbered and slept.

This symbolizes that they all had experienced the indwelling of the Holy Spirit, who comes to us at the new birth.

But only the wise still had oil in their jars — a separate personal portion. Only the wise had received the infilling of the Holy Spirit. Only the wise had hungered and thirsted for righteousness and been filled. They alone had paid the price. They received the fullness of the Holy Spirit, the fruit of the Holy Spirit, and the power to overcome sin in their lives. This is my portion, and it is your portion too.

Why were the others called *"foolish"*? Because they would not surrender self. They loved the things of the world and did not seek the deeper things of the Spirit. Their faith was cold or, at best, lukewarm.

The wise virgins took their entire portion so their lamps would show them the way. Jesus is the Way, and He is the Light of the world.

Since oil is symbolic of the Holy Spirit, the Bride has made herself ready, as these virgins made themselves ready. Let us receive our portion, which is apprehended through intimacy, a laid-down life, to become a laid-down lover of Jesus. We must awake quickly (see Psalm 17:15).

†

# 5. SPICE GARDEN

Who now strolls in His spice garden?

**Song of Songs 4:16**
> *Awake, north wind, and come, south wind!*
> *Blow on my garden that its fragrance may spread abroad.*

*Let my lover come into his garden
and taste its choice fruits.*

*Awake* means "to awake out of sleep or inactivity, to excite into action or attention."

**Song of Songs 4:12 (KJV)**

*A garden enclosed is my sister, my spouse; a spring shut up, a fountain sealed.*

She is uniquely His. Christ is in her. She is His Garden of Eden. A wall of stone around her makes her an enclosed garden. This garden is secluded from the public. It is for beauty's pleasure, not for commerce. She is His alone, shut up unto Him.

Verses 13 and 14 name the nine fruits of His garden:

**Song of Songs 4:13-14 (KJV)**

*Thy plants are an orchard of pomegranates, with pleasant fruits; camphire, with spikenard. Spikenard and saffron; calamus and cinnamon, with all trees of frankincense; myrrh and aloes, with all the chief spices:*

- *Pomegranates* are a symbol of pure thoughts and an open heart for the Lord, seeds of His words.
- *Camphire* and *spikenard* are symbols for the praise and worship of her perfume.

- *Cypress* points to the cross and all its workings. The cypress tree speaks of death. It will release the flow of the Holy Spirit, and it is costly.
- *Saffron* is yellow and speaks of gold, His divine nature. It is worth its weight in gold.
- *Calamus* and *cinnamon* are used in the anointing oil.
- In Psalm 45, the King's garments are scented with *myrrh* and *aloes*, which symbolize suffering love.
- Trees of *frankincense*, when cut, release their resin to flow out. *Aloes* have healing qualities.

This garden contains:

**Song of Songs 4:15 (KJV)**
*A fountain of gardens, a well of living waters, and streams from Lebanon.*

Then comes that wonderful verse 16:

**Song of Songs 4:16 (KJV)**
*Awake, O north wind; and come, thou south; blow upon my garden.*

The Bride calls for His breath of life. No matter if it is the negative or positive circumstances symbolic in these winds, she trusts that they are appointed by her King to develop the lovely fragrance of His garden and cause new life to flow out to the world. This was the heart of the ladies who attended the Emerging Bride Gathering, to have His Spirit blow upon us however He chose.

As the Bride, we are His spice garden. We invite Him into His garden where there are His fruits and spices to enjoy, to satisfy Him.

†

# 6. UNDER HIS WINGS

**Psalm 91:1-2 (KJV)**

*He that dwelleth [or sitteth] in the secret place of the most High [El-Elyon] shall abide under the shadow of the Almighty [Messiah, El-Shaddai].*
*I will say of the Lord [Jehovah], he is my refuge and my fortress: my God [Elohim]; in him will I trust [confide].*

This oil is created during a time of tribulation, and Psalm 91 is a hymn of trust filled with amazing and wonderful promises of security to those who trust in Yahweh. It is a psalm of light and life. I trust you now to read the entire psalm before going any further.

*Shall abide* means "to rest or repose."

*Under* signifies submission.

His shadow is a refuge and a protection.

*Refuge* means "to flee, trust, shelter."

*Fortress* means "a stronghold."

A *secret place* is "a standing or condition, a state of being, a reality."

We are protected by El-Elyon Himself.

**Psalm 91:4 (KJV)**

> *He shall cover thee with his feathers and under [submission] his wings [the Ark of the Covenant] shalt thou trust [flee for shelter].*

To *cover* means "to secure, protect."

*Feathers* means "a wing, in which lies the strength of a bird; collectively, members of His Body, His Bride."

All of these verses speak of the bridal canopy or *chuppah.* The Holy Spirit uses ancient Hebrew wedding traditions to convey this idea.

Yeshua, as the Bridegroom-King, has gone to prepare your bridal chamber. In present-day Jewish wedding ceremonies this phrase is still spoken.

Jesus said:

**John 14:2-3 (KJV)**

> *I go to prepare a place for you. And if I go and prepare a place for you, I will come again, and receive you unto myself; that where I am, there ye may be also.*

## Discerning the Meaning of the Oils

Our Bridegroom Yeshua has returned to His Father's house to prepare a bridal chamber. The Jews called such a chamber a *chador*. It was built onto the father's house. The Holy Spirit instructed us to build a *chuppah* for the women to stand under during the Emerging Bride Gathering.

In the original Hebrew, Psalm 19:6 speaks of the Bridegroom emerging from His *chuppah*. Joel 2:16 says, *"Let the bridegroom leave his room* (chedro) *and the Bride from her chamber* (chuppah). *"*

The following imagery was spoken at my own wedding from the book of Ruth:

In Ruth 3:9, Boaz (Jesus) is speaking and asks Ruth a question: *"Who are you?"*

She answers him, *"I am your servant Ruth. Spread the corner of your garment over me, since you are a kinsman-redeemer."*

Remember that in verse 9 of Psalm 91 we ask Him to spread His wings over us. In other words, she was saying, "Cover me, Boaz. Marry me."

We, as Christ's Betrothed One (like Ruth), are saying, "Redeem me, Boaz (Jesus). Redeem my spirit, soul, and body. Under Your wings I find refuge."

**Proverbs 18:10**
> *The name of the Lord is a strong tower;*
> *the righteous run to it and are safe."*

Wearing this oil reminds us of Him to whom we belong, the Bridegroom-King Yeshua. It is created in the secret place, or, as some have said, the "sacred" place.

†

# 7. TWO CAMPS OR MAHANAIM

**Song of Songs 6:13 (KJV)**
*Return, return, O Shulamite; return, return, that we may look upon thee.*

What will you see in the Shulamite? As it were the companies of two armies. As it were the dance of two companies.

This oil contains pomegranate, which stands for love, and myrtle, which stands for hiddenness. People don't know that you walk in two camps of angels. As intercessors, we birth things in secret, and oils are weapons in our war chest.

This oil was exciting for me because my personal experience of the Bridegroom/Bridal paradigm began with a dance. I still love to worship the Lord in the dance. As noted earlier, I was going through a very difficult trial in my life when the experience and revelation from the Song of Songs was given to me sovereignly. I had been diagnosed with breast cancer and was in for the fight for my life. One day, while pressing in to worship in my bedroom, the power and presence of the Holy Spirit came upon me, and I heard heavenly music in my spirit and around me.

Responding to this sound, I got up off the floor and moved in dance. At first it was very slow and lovely, like a ballet would feel. It then intensified into a warrior dance, with flashes of lightning all around me as I danced. I was healed from breast cancer while I danced (although the healing didn't manifest in my body until later). My healing testimony was confirmed when I went back to have surgery. That day angels came into my room to dance with me — two armies or companies gathered.

The full verse of Song of Songs 6:13 says:

**Song of Songs 6:13**

> *Come back, come back, O Shulamite;*
>   *come back, come back, that we may gaze on you.*
> *Why would you gaze upon the Shulamite*
>   *as on the daughter of Mahanaim?*

The King James Version renders these last two lines as:

> *What will ye see in the Shulamite? As it were the company of two armies.*

The Amplified Version further expands it to say:

> *What is there for you to see in the [poor little] Sh-*
> *ulammite? [And they answered] As upon a dance*
> *before two armies or a dance of Mahanaim.*

The Shulamite is in a place called Mahanaim, mean-ing "the place where Yahweh camps or dwells." The word *Mahanaim* means "two camps, two hosts, armies or encampments." This specific dance is a Victorious War Dance (see Exodus 15:19-21).

*Return* is mentioned in this verse four times. Four is the number of new creation, the cry of creation. In my own life, I was literally crying out to be made whole (a new creation), especially in my body. For me, it was truly a dance of victory.

In Genesis 32:1-2, Jacob called the place where he met the angels of God along his way Mahanaim. By that, he meant "this is Yahweh's camp."

**Song of Songs 7:1 (AMP)**

> *How beautiful are your feet in sandals, O*
> *queenly maiden.*

In the July 2010 Emerging Bride Gathering a group of Shulamite daughters heard the Lord sing over us. All through the night His angels — two camps of them — sang.

**Zephaniah 3:17 (KJV)**

> *The LORD thy God in the midst of thee is mighty;*
> *he will save, he will rejoice over thee with joy; ... he*
> *will joy over thee with singing.*

*"How beautiful are your feet* [walk]." According to Philippians 2:12-13, we are His workmanship. The workman is the Holy Spirit. Let our feet be shod with the Gospel of peace. According to *Strong's,* the Shulamite has the same name as her beloved (Solomon) — Peace. That must become our name too.

At the close of our Emerging Bride Gathering, while we were outside under the *chuppah,* we all simultaneously began to sing by the prompting of the Holy Spirit the scripture that says:

**Isaiah 55:12, KJV**

> *For ye shall go out with joy, and be led out with*
> *peace:*
> *the mountains and the hills shall break forth before*
> *you into singing,*
> *and all the trees of the field shall clap their hands.*

*The Bridal Dance of Christ*

Here is the interpretation given to me by the Holy Spirit of the dance I spoke of earlier:

## Threads of Gold

The Dancer: At the touch of the first string heard upon the harp, at the sound of the first note, she comes to life. My Spirit is upon her, and the Spirit brings life and liberty. The dancer begins to flow with My Spirit, oh so sweetly, oh so lovely, oh so graciously.

As the song arises, so does the Spirit lift her hands in praise and worship. Her eyes are turned upward. She sees only My face. As the music crescendos to new heights, so does My Spirit in her increase. It raises the dancer up into My presence, like a flower unfolding in the light.

As the Spirit moves through the music, the dancer begins to move and flow. Up, up, up into the heavenlies the fragrance of the flower ascends. The dancer is now one with Me. We are one, Creator and created, one in Spirit.

The dancer cannot hear or see anything but Me, her Beloved, her Lord. I am her All-in-All. She graciously sways her arms, her body. Her all becomes a sacrifice, a living sacrifice, a sacrifice of praise to Me.

A broken and contrite heart I see, for she is a worshipper of Me.

So listen, my dancer, my Beloved one.

Listen to My Spirit who calls to you.

As the heavenly sounds begin, listen and "Come Up."

"Come away with me, my Beloved, My Bride,

Let the Spirit and the Bride say, "Come"

The dancer is a type or symbol of all who watch, not with eyes of flesh, but with their spirits.

Through oneness with Me, My Bride's desire is complete. She only wants to please Me, not herself or man.

At the same time, I had a vision of a fully-opened rose, with a background of clear blue sky and petals from the rose falling. A holy fragrance from the Lord was being scattered. I was wearing a headband with twelve small white roses on it while I danced, and I was wearing a white linen dress, as a flower girl in a wedding goes before the bride to prepare the way.

Here comes the Bride!

†

# 8. AT HIS FEET SPECIALTY OIL

**Ruth 3:7-9**

*When Boaz had finished eating and drinking and was in good spirits, he went over to lie down at the end of the grain pile. Ruth approached quietly, uncovered his feet and lay down. In the middle of the night something startled the man, and he turned and discovered a woman lying at his feet.*

*"Who are you?" he asked.*

*"I am your servant Ruth," she said. "Spread the corner of your garment over me since you are a kinsman-redeemer."*

Another example of a bridal heart at Jesus' feet is found in Luke 10:

**Luke 10:38-40**

> *A woman named Martha opened her home to him [Jesus]. She had a sister called Mary, who sat at the Lord's feet listening to what He said. But Martha was distracted by all the preparations that had to be made. She came to him [Jesus] and asked, "Lord, don't you care that my sister has left me to do the work by myself? Tell her to help me!"*

Jesus did not rebuke Mary, but rather answered Martha that Mary had chosen the better part.

When the disciples were in a boat with Jesus during a raging storm at sea, they asked the Lord, *"Carest thou not that we perish?"* (Luke 4:38, KJV). Neither group was at rest and accused Jesus of not caring.

David sang:

**Psalm 27:4**

> *One thing I ask of the Lord,*
>   *that is what I seek:*
> *that I may dwell in the house of the Lord*
> *all the days of my life,*
> *to gaze upon the beauty of the Lord*
> *and to seek him in his temple.*

Both David and Mary wanted to know the Lord more than they wanted to know some information about Him. All we need is in Him.

Jesus taught:

**Matthew 5:6**

*Blessed are those who hunger and thirst for righteousness for they will be filled.*

We came together that weekend of the Emerging Bride Gathering to be filled with Him. Our only purpose was being with Him. Like Mary and David, we knew experientially that in Him we lived and moved and had our being. Now we waited at His feet in silence for His voice.

Jesus said:

**John 10:27 (KJV)**

*My sheep hear my voice, and I know them, and they follow me.*

**John 10:5**

*They will never follow a stranger; in fact, they will run away from him because they do not recognize his voice.*

On another occasion, Mary of Bethany proved her love for Jesus:

**Mark 14:3**

> *A woman came with an alabaster box of very expensive perfume, made of pure nard. She broke the jar and poured the perfume on his head [anointing Him for burial].*

The house was filled with the fragrance of that oil, and the fragrance rose, all over Him, and all over her.

No words were spoken. Rather, she demonstrated her heart in her deeds, in the scent, the fragrance, rather than in a speech, like the disciples had done. Mary broke her jar, her heart, her very being at His feet.

Not everyone was happy about that:

**Mark 14:4-5**

> *Some of those present were saying indignantly to one another, "Why this waste of perfume? It could have been sold for more than a year's wages and the money given to the poor. And they [not a few] rebuked her harshly.*

It was the custom at Passover to raise money by selling valuable things and giving that money to the poor. This woman chose to "waste" her perfume on Jesus.

Mary didn't hear her critics, as she went past them to His feet. She poured the oil on His head, down His body, and onto His feet that were so lovely to her as she sat near them.

Only Mary truly heard what the Lord was telling them about His coming death. Only Mary believed that whatever He said was true. He could not lie.

Mary demonstrated extravagant love versus respectability. She unfurled her hair (something never allowed in public without a scandal in those days) to wipe Jesus' feet (see John 12:3). It was all about Him. She held nothing back. She believed Him when He said He had to go away. She knew He was going to die soon, like a criminal, a horrible death. There would be no time later to anoint His body for burial. At the Passover meal, He would break the bread and say:

**Matthew 26:26**

*"Take and eat; this is my body."*

She broke the jar, acting out His soon-coming death. All the oil poured out.

At the Passover meal, He would then take the cup and say:

**Matthew 26:27**

*"Drink from it, all of you. This is my blood of the covenant, which is poured out for many for the forgiveness of sins."*

His holy and sinless blood would be spilled for them, for her, and she understood it. It was His death, but it was her death also, to loose the one she loved so deeply.

He had loved her first:

**John 3:16**

*For God so loved the world that he gave his one and only Son, Yeshua.*

Mary knew it before others did.

## A Feet Ministry

One day I was in deep prayer and worship while lying on the floor at Jesus' feet, and I had an open vision of those feet. I have no words to describe the beauty of them. I thought at the time about how people are always saying they want to see His face. I had been just as guilty as anyone in this regard. But now His feet were so wonderful that I thought to myself, "If they could just see how beautiful and magnificent His feet are, they would be surprised and satisfied," and from that time on, I have been called to a feet ministry, like Mary of Bethany, to Yeshua.

Since I saw His lovely feet, the Lord has asked me countless times to go to His children, especially pastors, and wash their feet. I believe He can trust us to do this work for Him only from the position of first being at His feet in worship and humility ourselves. Being sent from that posture allows us to go in His grace to wash the feet of others. Only humility can wash the pride away from others, as Jesus did for Peter.

I believe we should only be sent from lying at His feet to

**194**

do whatever we see our Father doing, and then we should run right back to His feet and continue our adoration. It is only in being a vessel that is broken in worship that we can be filled with His fragrance, to be poured out in love at the feet of our sisters and brothers. It is from this humble position that the Lord Jesus raises you up to look into His glorious face and hear His loving voice ask, "Who will go for us?" He then awaits your answer: "Here I am. Lord, send me."

**Song of Songs 7:1**
> *How beautiful your sandaled feet*
> *O prince's daughter!*

At His feet, we are transformed. Our walk is to minister to others in His strength and beauty, and not our own.

**Ephesians 6:14-15**
> *Stand firm then, ... and with your feet fitted with*
> *readiness that comes from the gospel of peace.*

✝

# 9. POSSESSING THE GATES

**Isaiah 45:1-3 (NKJV)**
> *Thus says the Lord to His anointed,*
> *To Cyrus, whose right hand I have held —*

> *To subdue nations before him*
> *And loose the armor of kings,*
> *To open before him the double doors,*
> *So that the gates will not be shut:*
>
> *"I will go before you*
> *And make the crooked places straight:*
> *I will break in pieces the gates of bronze*
> *And cut the bars of iron.*
> *I will give you the treasures of darkness*
> *And hidden riches of secret places,*
> *That you may know that I, the Lord,*
> *Who call you by name,*
> *Am the God of Israel."*

We have gates in us that need to be possessed, removed, or cleansed. We must possess our own gates before we can possess other gates for the Lord.

What is a gate? Simply put, it is a way in. Gates, then, are spiritual ways, or paths, to the blessings the Father has promised us. Many of our gates need repaired or strengthened. They have been closed, double-minded, or destroyed by wrong thinking.

According to *Strong's,* the meaning of *possess* is: "O.T. 3423 = *yarash*, means "to occupy (by driving out previous tenants, and possessing in their place); by implication, to seize, to inherit, impoverish, to ruin." The meaning of *gate* is: "O.T.

8179 *sha'ar* (shah'-ar) from O.T. 8176 its original sense, an opening i.e. door or gate. KJV — city, door, gate, port."

**Psalm 24:7**

> *Lift up your heads, o you gates*

This speaks of entrances.

Rebekah was to possess the gates of her enemies:

**Genesis 24:60 (NKJV)**

> *And they blessed Rebekah and said to her:*

> *"Our sister, may you become*
> *The mother of thousands of ten thousands;*
> *And may your descendants possess*
> *The gates of those who hate them."*

In Jewish homes, this blessing is still spoken over daughters on *Shabbat* (the Sabbath).

The first ingredient in Possessing the Gates oil is found in the To Contend oil.

To Contend: Yahweh says He will contend with those who contend with us.

The word *contend* means: "O.T. 7378 riyb (reeb) root; 'to toss, grapple mostly figuratively, to wrangle i.e. hold a controversy (by implication) to defend.' KJV — adversary, chide, complain, debate plead, rebuke strive."

The second ingredient is cardamon. Cardamon brings stability to the oil. The Word of God does this in us. It holds the promises of Yahweh.

The third ingredient is hyssop. Hyssop represents the blood of Yeshua that purchased our right to the gate (see Exodus 12:22-24).

The fourth ingredient is benzion. This represents the voice of the Lord that lines our souls up with the will of Abba and releases His voice and His authority through us.

The fifth ingredient is galbanum. This was one of the ingredients in the holy anointing oil for the Tabernacle and Temple. It is a vermicide, a fumigant. It is a tenacious and very powerful fighting oil.

**Isaiah 22:23 (KJV)**

*And I will fasten him as a nail in a sure place; and he shall be for a glorious throne to his father's house.*

The sixth ingredient is Throne Room oil. This establishes the presence of the throne of the Lord and His cherubim.

The seventh is Priestly Bride.

The eight is panoply, which means "armored and fully dressed for battle."

When we use Possessing the Gates oil, the Lord will recognize us because it is the hidden fragrance of the Bride who worships Him the way He wants. He will always recognize His own scent.

In Possessing the Gates oil, there is a kiss of the fragrance of neroli that comes from the bitter orange tree, the bridal scent, and some Angelica, the presence of angels.

Lastly is the color amber, representing the holiness of Yahweh.

The authority to legislate and magistrate is on this oil. It signifies having dominion. *Dominion*: "domain, supreme authority, sovereignty, an order of angels, celestial hierarchy, absolute ownership." A synonym is "power." As we set out to possess or take dominion of the gates held captive by the enemy, we can be assured that Yahweh has sent angelic hosts before and behind (the rear-guard) to detonate and obliterate everything in our path. It shall be as it was declared to the prophet Jeremiah:

**Jeremiah 1:10**

*See, today, I appoint you over nations and kingdoms to uproot and tear down, to destroy and overthrow [the plots and plans of the enemy. Then] to build and to plant.*

✝

# 10. AWAKEN BRIDE

The last oil discussed here will be about the process of this particular oil, unlike the last oil number #9. I wrote mostly about the meanings of the ingredients used. The creator of this specialty oil gave me the following:

That she poured and simmered the oil for twenty-four months. That it is a unique blend of twenty-four drops of precious fragrance, blended in an almond base, kissed with honey and My Ishi. It was specifically released to Awaken His Bride Ministries in His timing in 2012.

Three scriptures were given for our interpretation:

**Song of Songs 5:2**

*I slept, but my heart was awake.*

**Jeremiah 1:11**

*I see the branch of an almond tree.*

The almond base speaks of the call to awake or bud.

**Isaiah 52:1**

*Awake, Awake, ... clothe yourself with strength.*

The number 24 speaks of the Priestly Bride for it speaks of heavenly authority (see Revelation 4:4).

Being under the jurisdiction of God, I had a vision at this same time I would like to share regarding being awakened. I (representing His Bride) was in bed asleep. An alarm clock was on the bedside table, and it began to sound. I (the Bride) reached over and tried to shut the alarm clock off, but as hard as I tried I could not find the snooze button. It had been removed. I then woke up in the vision.

It is time to be awakened. No more slumbering or sleeping. Wake up!

†

# CANADA ARISE

One of the first specialty oils poured after this gathering was for our neighboring country of Canada. The Holy Spirit named it "Canada Arise." Here is what the apothecary wrote after it came forth:

"This oil came forth so deliberately and with precision. These are your words, O Canada. 'Come forth with a deliberate focus and with precision.' " The essences used for your oil were the following:

- *Rose* (three kinds) for the fragrance of the Rose of Sharon
- *Neroli* for the bridal scent for His awakened/emerging Bride
- *Amber,* like the fiery presence around Ezekiel's throne
- *Balm of Gilead,* one drop, which is your own unique mother's drop, like Rachel weeping for her children. Incidentally, the drop used had its origin in Canada. There was a gentle weeping for the awe of God's purpose for Canada. It was created in Victorie (victory) for your nation."

†

Gloria also has two new oils given to the Bride as of the Jewish year 5773 or 2013. For Israel, the oil is Strengthen the Gates, and it is based on Psalm 147:13. For the United States, the new oil, based on Isaiah 58:9-12, is Repair the Gates.

Chapter 49

# The Importance of the Scents

WHY IS SCENT SO important to me? Cynthia, a friend of mine (although we've only spoken by phone so far), is a biblical ancient oil apothecary, and she has taught and studied these oils for decades, as well as gone to the Holy Land numerous times. (I am more than a little envious.) She explained to me that only the sense of smell wasn't defiled in the Garden of Eden. The Jewish people believe that Messiah will return to the smell of His own scent, and I happen to agree. This may be why there is such increased awareness these days, both good and bad, regarding aromatherapy around the world. New-Agers like it, but it is also biblical. These scents were first released in the Garden of Eden.

Satan wants to try and rob the sense of smell for himself, just as he robbed man of other elements in the Garden of Eden. There he perverted sight (the woman saw that the fruit was good to eat). He perverted hearing (accusing Yahweh of withholding: *"Did God say?"*). He perverted touch (Eve gave the fruit to her husband, and he touched it and ate it. Did she pluck off the fruit from the tree herself or was it given to her by the evil one?)

Hearing also became perverted when Adam and Eve heard their Father's voice and hid from Him for the first time. Satan also perverted taste (it was no longer good to eat or did not taste good to them).

Now he wants to rob us of the blessing of heavenly smell, but God is restoring the scents of Heaven to us. We are His scent (sent) ones. Thank God for anointed apothecaries.

Chapter 50

# *Preparations for the Chuppah*

THE *CHUPPAH* ITSELF LOOKED magnificent. Everyone had come together with different giftings to prepare it with flowers and greenery, lace linen cloths, and silks, all draped around the poles. Some of the provisions for the *chuppah* had come with the group from Pennsylvania. It was then assembled, and once this was accomplished, everyone had a part in decorating it.

We had it set up outdoors, and it was July and hot for Upstate New York. The top was open to the skies, so that we could see the moon and stars. We had a beautiful oriental rug inside on the grass for the ladies to lie or kneel on before the Lord.

Gloria had brought specially-made sprays to anoint the inside of the *chuppah,* and it smelled awesome. In fact, it was absolutely intoxicating.

Angels were waiting outside the *chuppah* to watch and take names. It was all so thrilling, like waiting on the eve of your wedding night, hanging out with your sisters, and talking. It was hard to fall asleep, but finally sleep came.

That next morning the sun rose to greet us with a huge smile. This was the day we had been waiting for, and we were ready and eager to experience it.

Chapter 51

# *Intimacy in the Chuppah*

OUR PRIVATE TIME IN the chuppah was reserved for the last day. We decided, by mutual consent, to keep private whatever transpired between each of us and the Lord at that time.

We each had our own time with Him in the *chuppah,* talking with Him and listening to Him. This is the exact opposite of what would happen in a true Jewish wedding. In that case, the time inside the *chuppah* would be public, for all to hear and witness what is being vowed. But ours was not an actual wedding, just a rehearsal, a heartfelt covenant commitment, although it was still authentic and genuine.

While each woman took her turn inside the *chuppah,* she had the opportunity to read once again the *ketubah, or* Jewish wedding vows. Wikipedia describes the *ketubah* as follows:

> A *ketubah* (Hebrew: "written thing"; pl. *ketubot*) is a special type of Jewish prenuptial agreement.

It is considered an integral part of a traditional Jewish marriage, and outlines the rights and responsibilities of the groom, in relation to the bride. Nevertheless, there is no agreement in modern times as to the monetary worth of the *ketubah*, and its enforceability even in Jewish courts is in question even in theory; in practice it is never enforced. [10]

My husband Roy had prepared beautiful copies of the *ketubah*, and each woman had a copy to take with her inside the *chuppah*. On each form was a place to sign your name, if you agreed with the terms of the vows and came into covenant with the Bridegroom Yeshua (see Ezekiel 16:8-14).

One of our sisters kept notes on all that was said and done during those very special days, and some women chose to reveal what had happened to them in the *chuppah*. These have been included in the appendices.

One incident I feel free to write about was a miracle that happened to one of the younger brides there. She had asked a friend she knew to accompany her inside the *chuppah* and began to ask questions about the baptism of the Holy Spirit, and her friend was able to show her, both in the Word and experientially, what it is. This calmed her fears, and the younger women asked to be filled, or baptized, in the Holy Spirit, and she was — right then and there. Oh my, the joy that exploded in and through her and all of the rest of us was such a gift from our heavenly Father! The angels were ecstatic, twirling and whirling in joyful praise. Hearts were healed and filled with God's power and love.

As the night wore on various ministries were taking place simultaneously. No one wanted the evening to end. Eternal relationships were being birthed by the Holy Spirit, and all felt included. At the end of the book, you can read testimonies from some of the brides in attendance and be blessed.

We exchanged the gifts that Margreit had bought for each one of the brides, like a bridal shower gift or wedding gift.

When each one had finished having their private turn in the *chuppah,* they came inside and found these gifts on a table. They were encouraged to choose the gift that spoke to them or had some special meaning for them. (The gifts were purposely not wrapped so that we could see what they were.) Later, not one thought they had picked the wrong gift, and each loved what they had received. The Holy Spirit is the perfect Gift-Giver.

Chapter 52

# *Experiencing Mahanaim*

OUR JOYOUS CELEBRATION EVENT continued, as each woman fell at Jesus' feet in adoration and humility. One of the younger women present even consented to wear an actual white wedding gown and danced as we joined her in the dance of Mahanaim.

As noted earlier, Song of Songs 6:13 explains this dance as a company or dance of two armies. Mahanaim was the place where Yahweh camped or dwelt, and the dance is called a Victorious War Dance.

The name *Mahanaim* means "two armies, or camps," the actual dance means "to twirl or whirl in a circular manner, showing great exaltation publicly with joy and gladness." (Two armies [#4264] = army, angels, stars, battle camp.) So we all joined hands, danced, twirled, and were free to express, in any fashion we desired, our joy in this joining into oneness.

Of course this went on for some time, and many, if not all, were receiving personal ministry. Some were receiving prophetic words. Others were being healed physically, emotionally, and relationally. Whatever their need was, it was healed with laughter and love.

One sister, Linda from Kansas City received ministry from the Holy Spirit in a unique way, as did most of the other women there. Linda was in a Holy Spirit bridal wave and was receiving a great impartation of a furious tidal wave of Bride-Bridegroom love. This was to be taken back home with her and released wherever the Lord showed her.

By now, she (and all the rest of us) were pretty much drunk in the Spirit (filled to overflowing with the glory and love of His manifest presence). Many of the ladies were lying quietly on the floor soaking in the glory and weeping quietly tears of joy, gratitude, and thanksgiving.

Chapter 53

# The End of a Perfect Few Days

AS MUCH AS WE wanted to delay the inevitable, later that day the women had to begin packing their suitcases for their trips home the next day. Some were flying and had to leave earlier to get to the airport on time. Most were driving home, but to different states and some longer distances than others, so they still needed to pack and rest a little for the long drive home — to Pennsylvania, Virginia, California, Missouri, Canada and also nearby in New York. Somehow, by a miracle, we did settle down for the night late into the AM. But then, about 1:00 AM, the Holy Spirit began to reveal glorious things to different women. These are recorded and included in the appendices.

Those were glorious days.

Part V

# The Aftermath

Chapter 54

# A Serious Transition

TRANSITIONS ARE OFTEN DIFFICULT, and as we all parted at the farm I sensed that this one might be especially difficult. We had been led to form Key Ministries, and God had blessed that. Now, however, we had a new mandate, a new focus, a new commissioning. God had revealed to us many wonderful things about the emerging bride, and we now must share these things with others.

When Key Ministries was first birthed, we went to the Heflin campground in Ashland, Virginia, and Jane Lowder spoke a word of prophecy over us. One part of that prophecy said that when we got crowned, as in playing checkers, we would then move in liberty in all directions. This happened the weekend we were together, and then everyone went in all directions back to their own homes — north, south, east and west — crowned and with a scepter.

So what was the future of Key Ministries? Suddenly it was no longer visible, and yet those keys were alive and viable within us. We still had our right to the keys of the Kingdom, but they had to take their place beside the many other keys we had now been given. We had the keys, and now the Lord had shown us how to use them correctly, with wisdom and understanding.

Those keys were not to be discarded. Nor would they disappear. They were still an integral part of us.

Chapter 55

# *Confirmations*

TRANSITION IS OFTEN DIFFICULT precisely because we feel more secure in the old than in the new and often hesitate to make the necessary adjustments. But were we right about the serious changes we felt the Spirit calling us to make?

Shortly after the sisters attending the Emerging Bride Gathering had dispersed, each going back to her own home, the Holy Spirit spoke prophetically to me again. Then He gave me some amazing miracles as confirmations of what He had done in those days.

I went to the farm to wash the towels we had used, and while I was there, a thunderstorm, very unusual for the north country, came up. It became very dark with thunder clouds, and the wind began to blow. This might be typical in Missouri, but not here. The thunderings got very loud outside, and as I was working inside I heard the Holy Spirit say to me, "Go outside." I did.

I was led to go around back to where the *chuppah* was still set up, but as I started to go around the corner, the rain began to pour. I stayed in the rain, and when I reached the part of the backyard where we were inside the *chuppah*, it really poured, and the black clouds were amazing. All I could do was worship, and I could smell the fragrance of the oils. They must have been re-released or activated by the rain. It was sooo fragrant and intoxicating!

After a while I was soaking wet and worshipping the Father and suddenly in the midst of all black foreboding thunderclouds was an opening with a huge gate, and that gate was also opening. It was formed by white and pink clouds. All around was darkness, but in the center was God's glory shining through. Then, after about four or five minutes, it all closed back to just all black clouds again.

I was led to take a little walk. Walking down the country road in front of the house, I looked to the east and saw the most vivid, colorful, double rainbow. Since I am a Messianic Jew, rainbows speak loudly to me about covenant and the promises of God. I rejoiced seeing the double rainbow so clearly, and it confirmed to me that God had placed His approval on our Emerging Bride Gathering. I danced down the road to the farmhouse, ecstatic with joy.

The next day it happened again, only this time I saw a single rainbow on the same county road. Later, when I drove home I took Highway 37, and I saw a second double rainbow. It was just as brilliant and clear as the others, nothing faint or foggy or hard to see. Needless to say, I was beginning to wonder why I was seeing so many rainbows so close together. It was awesome to witness.

On the third day, I saw my third single rainbow. It was straight across from the farmhouse in a field. It was so real that I felt like I could just run across the street and step inside the colors of it. It was amazingly close, and the colors were amazingly dynamic. I cried and laughed with excitement and was humbled that we, as a group, had pleased the Lord, for Him to demonstrate to us this great sign.

Then, lastly, as I drove home once more on Highway 37 I could hardly believe my eyes. As I came over a large hill, directly over my house was yet another double rainbow. This brought the total to eight rainbows that I had seen with my own eyes in three days after experiencing an outstanding, overwhelming, intimate time with our Bridegroom, King Yeshua, the Father, and the Holy Spirit, with the holy angels watching and smiling with approval, acceptance, and love.

I was exploding, bursting with joy, praise, and worship flowing freely from my spirit and mouth: "Thank You, thank You, thank You, a hundred times, Abba God. *Merci*."

I quickly ran inside and phoned Roy at work, explaining to him that it looked like we had McDonalds golden arches over our house, and we could just drive into them. But these arches were so much better because they represented God's promises.

Our Father is the Covenant Keeper, the Promises Keeper, the one and only who cannot lie. He is truth.

**Numbers 23:19**

*God is not a man, that he should lie,*
*nor a son of man, that he should change his mind.*

After telling Roy the exciting news I phoned all the women I could reach and told them the miracles of the rainbows our Father had sent to encourage and remind us that the experience we'd had together was now authenticated with signs and wonders. Counting the double rainbows as two each, there were eight in all (eight signifying new beginnings).

*Covenant* is such a sacred word in Hebraic and biblical thinking, yet in the Western world it is something so casual. The definition of *covenant* is "a binding, indissoluble agreement between two people or two groups that contains promises made on the part of each to the other." Biblically speaking, a covenant cannot be broken.

Contracts are for a limited time (which is what we are witnessing more and more in the world now and even the church) while a covenant is an eternal agreement.

The purpose for all these women coming to the Emerging Bride Gathering was to get to understand covenant relationships experientially, that is beyond head knowledge. This was our collective desire for one another, as well as the desire of Father, Yeshua, and the Holy Spirit.

We began a deeper revelation and grasped the fact that it would only be maintained by grace. Each of us went home to apply these principals and experiences with our families, husbands, and friends.

Chapter 56

# *"Awaken the Bride"*

ABOUT A MONTH OR so later, one morning in August or September, I woke up hearing someone say to me, "Awaken the Bride." When I was fully awake, I realized it was the Holy Spirit, and He spoke that phrase to me again: "Awaken the Bride." I pondered this for some days and studied the Word about being awakened, but nothing seemed to bear witness to me about the revelation of truth I was seeking.

Gloria and I spoke by phone then, and she told me that while on her way to work on the train she had heard the words *Talitha cumi* and *Tabitha*. It took me weeks, even months, of waiting on the Lord to get the understanding of what the Lord was trying to say to us through this name and these words. What could this possibly have to do with awakening the Bride?

In the beginning, I treated the matter like homework and studied Hebrew commentaries and biblical definitions. I found:

**Psalm 17:15 (AMP)**

*As for me, I will continue beholding Your face in righteousness (rightness, justice, and right standing with You); I shall be fully satisfied, when I awake [to find myself] beholding Your form [and having sweet communion with You].*

The Hebrew word translated *awake* here is *koum.* It means "to get up, lift up, to rise — to incite, to stir up, to make stand." As I was writing these words, a very strong essence or aroma of almond was being released in the room. I could smell it profusely, and it was not going away, and no one was baking cookies or other pastries nearby using almond extract. It was one of those spiritual prophetic experiences.

I looked up the word *almond* in my *Strong's Concordance.* It said: "#8247 from #8245, a tree or nut being in earliest bloom." "#8245, to be alert i.e. sleepless, to be on the lookout (whether good or ill), watch, wake, hasten."

**Ecclesiastes 12:5 (KJV)**

*The almond tree shall flourish.*

**Jeremiah 1:11**

*"I see the branch of an almond tree," I replied.*

**Song of Songs 8:4 (KJV)**

> *I charge you, O daughters of Jerusalem, that ye
> stir not up, nor awake my love, until he please.*

God's voice, His Word by His Holy Spirit, and the Spirit of prophesy, which is the testimony of Yeshua (see Revelation 19:10) guided me and began to wake me up. This call was to awaken *me* to rise up, go forth, and awaken the Bride to all she had either forgotten or had never been taught in the first place. The Holy Spirit reminded me about seeing the eight rainbows, and taught me new revelations, meanings for me to go now and awaken the Bride.

The brilliance of the rainbows represents glorified and sanctified believers while worshipping Yahweh. The shining colors do not come from the rainbow itself. A rainbow merely displays the light rays from the sun, refracted through the water vapor and reflected by the clouds. So it is with us, the glorified Church.

God said:

**Genesis 9:13**

> *I set my rainbow in the clouds, and it will be the sign
> of the covenant between me and the earth.*

This was a covenant with Noah and his sons, a seal of Yahweh's promise, representing His destiny for those nations, ethnic groups, cultures, and languages. Their destiny would be fulfilled in those called out from every nation, the *ecclesia* (see Revelation 7:9). In 2 Corinthians 3:18-4:6, Paul declares that we reflect the glory of Yahweh shining through the face of Yeshua.

There is a rainbow around Yahweh's throne (see Revelation 4:3).

I had a lot to learn.

Chapter 57

# A Vessel of Deliverance

**Matthew 24:37**

> *As it was in the days of Noah, so it will be at the coming of the Son of Man.*

JUST AS THE RAINBOW was a covenant with Noah, the ark he built was a vessel of deliverance for him and his sons, and that is all relevant to our day.

Noah wasn't interested in what the wicked were doing, but what Yahweh was doing. It was the wicked who were taken away in the destruction of the flood, not the righteous (Noah and his family). The righteous were left behind to inherit the new earth.

Yahweh was not sitting by idly. He was busy building a vessel of deliverance, an ark that would save Noah and his family, and He was using Noah to do this (see Genesis 6).

It was Yahweh, not Noah, who knew how to build the ark. Noah was just a willing and obedient servant.

As the psalmist prayed:

**Psalm 90:12**

*Teach us to number our days aright,*
*that we may gain a heart of wisdom.*

Abba God is building a house of living stones, a habitation of Yahweh through the Spirit. This will be a mighty vessel of deliverance in the time of the judgment of the last days (judgment for the wicked).

In case you just missed it, that was the sound of the shofar (trumpet) waking you up to the truth. The thing that joins God's people together into one Church is not the doctrine, denomination, traditions, great preaching, wonderful music and singing, or fine buildings. It is the anointing. That anointing can be found in living rooms, store buildings, tents, garages, even a stable, or chicken coop. As long as the anointing is present, you'll find a people moving on in Yahweh into the oneness of the Spirit.

Noah's Ark was one vessel fifty cubits wide, the number of the anointing. This is what we all experienced at the farm in New York at the Emerging Bride Gathering. And I personally believe this is why the Lord used this sign and wonder, the rainbows, to remind us of Noah's covenant and that ours cannot be broken by the Father. We are now that mighty vessel of deliverance for all mankind, to become His Mercy Seat so that when others meet us they will see and find the mercy of Yahweh (no more floods to destroy all His beloved children).

When the enemy comes in like a flood, the Lord raises up a standard against him, and you and I are that standard, beloved. His banner over us is love, not hatred.

Chapter 58

# *Talitha Cumi and Tabitha*

NOW LET'S GET BACK to the phrases Gloria heard —
*Tabitha cumi* and *Tabitha*.

In the Bible there are two incidents in which a young
girl was involved. One, with the Lord Yeshua, is found in
Mark 5:14, and another is found in Acts 9:36-42 (where
Peter is helping a young girl). In both cases, the young girls
in question had died.

Let us look first at the case with Jesus, where we can glean
various lessons for the awakened Bride.

In the book of Mark 5:36-43 we can read the first
account, a scenario played out before many, including the ruler of the synagogue named Jairus, and his
daughter who, according to what he, Jesus and everyone
else within earshot was told, had died. The only people
allowed into the young girl's room now, where her
body had been laid out, was Peter, James, and John, his
brother (see verse 37).

Yeshua's only instructions to the ruler Jairus is in verse 36:

Mark 5:36
*Do not be afraid. Only believe.*

In the next two verses, Yeshua rebuked the tumult and the people weeping. He understood their lack of trust or faith in Him. He told them all that the little girl was not dead but sleeping (see verse 39).

In the next verse, we see that the people were not hopeful or humble. It says that they laughed and jeered at Jesus. But He put them out. Doubt and unbelief kills faith and hope.

Then, taking the child's father and mother and others who were with Him (not against Him), He went in where the little girl was lying.

**Mark 5:41-43 (AMP)**
*Gripping her [firmly] by the hand, He said to her, Tabitha cumi — which translated is, Little Girl, I say to you arise [from the sleep of death]. And instantly the girl got up and started walking around — for she was twelve years old. And they were utterly astonished and overcome with amazement. And He strictly commanded and warned them that no one should know this.*

Next, Jesus expressly told the people to give the girl something to eat. Why? In this same way, when He had risen from the dead, He ate with His disciples, and this proved to them that He was indeed alive and not just a ghost (in spirit form only).

In *Strong's Concordance* #G5000, we find the reference to the name "Tabitha = female gazelle, the name of the woman Peter raised from the dead." That number 5000 was what started my entire journey about Peter and this account with Tabitha.

Chapter 59

# My Bridal Dress

THAT NUMBER HAD APPEARED in another way, in a dream. In an earlier part of the book I described a dream I had about receiving a new wedding dress from My Abba God. You can read the rest of the story back there, but now I am adding a missing element. In the dream I was in a wedding salon picking out new gowns, but couldn't find any I particularly loved. The sales woman kept asking me if I could afford such an expensive dress. I answered, "Yes, my Father is paying for the dress." She asked me this on three different occasions, and I had to reassure her: "Yes, I can afford the more expensive dress because I'm not paying for it. My Father is."

Finally, she believed me and took me into a totally different place in the bridal salon and showed me exquisite, one-of-a-kind dresses. I said, "Oh, yes, this is more like what I was looking for."

And then I found my dress. The design was perfect for me, but the dress needed a little alteration to fit me perfectly. She told me to wait for three days and then call her back to see if the dress was ready. I agreed.

But patience is not my strong suit. I like to see my gifts as soon as possible and sometimes find it difficult to wait. (I've been doing much better with this in recent years.) I went back to the wedding salon and asked if my dress was ready to be picked up. The sales lady said, "No, I told you we have to custom fit it for you, and it takes time. We will call you when it's finished."

As I was leaving the shop, I felt impressed to look behind a small curtain, and there was an old man working on my dress. He locked eyes with me, and I saw that He was working on attaching by hand a multitude of white pearls all over the dress.

He looked at me, smiled, and said "Your intercession is almost completed. Then the dress is yours." Instinctively I knew He was the Holy Spirit working on my dress. I left, thrilled to know the dress was close to being completed.

On the way out, the sales lady reminded me that the dress cost $5,000, and for many years to come I waited to get the understanding of that number.

I am a big biblical numbers person, and I love studying the significance of biblical numbers, but nothing that I heard or read seemed to satisfy me or truly bear witness with my spirit on this subject.

Every source I have concerning the number 5 associates the idea of God's grace and life. The idea of preparation is also seen in the Hebrew word *chamash*, the word for five. *Chamash* means "to prepare or be made ready." The point being made here is that the wedding dress is being prepared by God's grace and mercy. His unearned gift of grace (#5) is given to prepare us for our ultimate glorification. God sees this process in five steps found in Romans 8:29-31:

> *For whom he did foreknow,* (1) *he also did predestinate* (2) *to be conformed to the image of his Son, that he might be the firstborn among many brethren. Moreover whom he did predestinate, them he also called* (3): *and whom he called, them he also justified* (4): *and whom he justified, them he also glorified* (5). (KJV)

As for *Talitha cumi* and *Tabitha,* I looked both of them up in *Strong's Concordance.* My understanding was quickened when my sisters suggested that I look up the number 5000 to see what it referred to. I did this (and they did too), and, low and behold, there it was in both of these two stories, Jesus raising a girl to life again and Peter doing the same. In Mark's story, it was number 5008, and number 5000 in the Hebrew concordance.

Before continuing, here are some thoughts I wrote down years ago while pondering the wedding dress:

*Revelations on the Wedding Dress:*

- The Pearls on the dress I saw in my dream are prayers made in silence, unseen, quiet, and barren.

- The Holy Spirit picks up one single gold thread. This gold thread will be used to hold each pearl in place.
- Pearls can be multi-purposed. Prayers and intercessions, too, are multi-purposed.
- Some people are pearls of great price.
- What are the threads of gold? Graces.
- It takes a special grace to sit in God's presence and wait, just wait, in a wilderness of barrenness, with nothing, no emotions, no thrills.
- The gold thread is picked up again, and the Holy Spirit begins to weave it, embroidering on the dress.
- What will hold the wedding gown together? Grace.
- We sit in silence and wait. Why?
- Nothing comes, no one speaks, only quiet!
- Our soul cries out, no, screams out, inside us. "Where are You, God?"
- Each bride has her own unique wedding dress style, created in her quiet, intimate time with Him. Collectively they form one magnificent glorious dress.

Beloved, don't doubt in the dark what Yahweh has shown you in the light.

He may leave you in silence. When we ask, "Where are You, Lord?" what does the Lord do? He withdraws the sense of His presence from us to draw us out of ourselves to find Him. In this way, He has aroused us by His silence to seek Him more diligently.

Chapter 60

# *Faith and Love*

IN PETER'S CASE, AFTER the Lord was crucified and then resurrected, it was hard for the disciples to fully comprehend. When Mary Magdalene went into the tomb and saw that the stone had been removed from the entrance, she ran to Simon Peter and John and said:

**John 20:2**

> *"They have taken the Lord out of the tomb, and we don't know where they have put him!"*

So Peter and John started for the tomb. Both were running, but John outran Peter and reached the tomb first.

John bent down and looked at the strips of linen lying there but did not go in. Then Simon Peter, who was behind him, arrived and went into the tomb. He saw the linen strips lying there, as well as the burial cloth that had been on Jesus' head.

In this incident, Peter, to me, represents faith, for he did something that John had *not* done.

John, to me, represents love. He called himself the disciple *"whom Jesus loved"* (John 13:23). John's whole life and message and the Gospel that bears his name were about love. Why would it be any different now?

John reached the tomb first, but only looked in. Peter, however, was not satisfied until he had gone inside to see for himself. *"Faith ... worketh by love"* (Galatians 5:6, KJV). John (love) left a deposit of divine love for Peter, to see by faith and believe.

Names were important in biblical times, and they still are today. Peter (faith) walked on water. His name also meant "rock or stone." When Yeshua went to raise Jairus' daughter to life, He took in with him three disciples. They were:

1. Peter ("stone," "faith")
2. James (whose name means "replaced"), and
3. John (whose name means "God's grace").

So, using these names as an illustration, we could say that the stone of death, by faith, had been replaced by God's grace in resurrecting Jairus' daughter for the glory of Yahweh.

Now it is later, and the disciples have been locked away in fear. Suddenly Jesus came in, stood among them, and said, *"Peace be with you"* (Luke 24:36). He showed them His hands and side. The disciples were overjoyed. Wouldn't you be? He then breathed on them and said, *"Receive the Holy Spirit"* (John 20:22).

Lastly, the Acts narrative says:

**Acts 9:36**

> *In Joppa there was a disciple named Tabitha (which, when translated, is Dorcas), who was always doing good and helping the poor.*

Tabitha became ill and died, and her body was washed and placed in an upstairs room. It was the custom in those days, for health reasons, to prepare a body for burial as quickly as possible. The Law demanded it.

Peter was sent for, and he came. What he found was interesting:

**Acts 9:39**

> *All the widows stood around him, crying and showing him the robes and other clothing that Dorcas had made while she was still with them.*

Just as Jesus had ordered everyone to leave the room, Peter cleared the room and began to pray. Then:

**Acts 9:40-42**

> *Turning toward the dead woman, he said, "Tabitha, get up."*

*She opened her eyes, and seeing Peter, she sat up.*
*He took her by the hand and helped her to her feet.*
*Then he called the believers and the widows and*
*presented her to them alive. This became known all*
*over Joppa, and many people believed in the Lord.*

The Hebrew *ko-maw* means "to help lift up again, appointed, arise, round up, and strengthen [what Peter was now doing for others], succeed, decree, confirm, and ordain." All of these words are what our Abba Father is declaring over us, His Maiden Bride, who is even now being awakened to who she is and to Whom she belongs.

# To Wake Up from a Dream

I WAS TAUGHT IN the 1980s by the Holy Spirit that I was an amethyst stone, a part of the twelfth foundation stone of the New Jerusalem. Amethyst means "one who has awakened from a dream." We wake up from our own dreams to know His dream. Yahweh's Dream is marriage for His Son Yeshua.

Among other things, amethyst stones were used to inlay the bottom of wine goblets used in weddings and other celebrations. The purple stone made the color of the wine deeper, richer, and purer.

The number twelve is the number of government, and the age of the maiden raised to life was also twelve. It is time for the government of Yahweh to wake up. Arise and Shine!

**Isaiah 60:1**

*Arise, shine, for your light has come,*
*and the glory of the Lord rises upon you.*

**Zechariah 8:23 (AMP)**

*Thus says the Lord [Adonai] of hosts: In those days [today] ten men out of all languages of the nations [gentiles] shall take hold of the robe of him who is a Jew [Hebrew], saying, Let us go with you, for we have heard that God [Yahweh] is with you.*

Wake up, Beloved Bride!

Chapter 62

# Would the Real Elaine Please Stand Up

IN THE 1950S THERE was a popular TV show called *I've Got a Secret*. Several contestants would come on at once, all claiming to be the same person. For instance, the first one might say, "I am John Jones." The second one and each one that followed would say exactly the same thing, that *they* were John Jones. The members of the permanent panel of judges who were blindfolded would then ask each contestant questions to see if they could detect from the clues given in the answers which one was the real John Jones. At the end of a certain time period, they would vote for the contestant they believed to be genuine.

Eventually the game show host would say, with great drama and fanfare, "Now, would the real John Jones please stand up." The panel members would take off their blindfolds to see if they had guessed correctly. Everyone would hold their breath in anticipation, as one or two contestants would pretend like they were going to stand up, until finally the real person stood. Often the panel would be surprised, everyone would applaud, and the real person would be rewarded for their efforts.

I would always play along with the judges on the panel, and by the end of each episode, a lot of anxiety would have built up inside of me. I would be thinking to myself, "Yes, would the real Elaine please stand up now so we can see her." Later I would wonder why these emotions ran so deep in me. Didn't I know my own identity, who I really was?

Since I was still a child at the time, I didn't pursue it any further then, but it stayed with me. I felt like Snow White who had been poisoned by the wicked witch and had fallen asleep and was waiting for my Prince (Jesus) to come and awaken me to who I really was. I slept and waited a long time to be awakened.

**Psalm 27:10**
> *Though my father and mother forsake me,*
> *the Lord will receive me.*

**Psalm 10:14**
> *You, O God, ... are the helper of the fatherless.*

**Psalm 109:22**
> *For I am poor and needy,*
> *and my heart is wounded within me.*

The purpose of this account is to tell you that it has taken me these many years to be awakened to His love for me.

**2 Corinthians 1:3-4**

> *Praise be to the God and Father of our Lord Jesus Christ, the Father of compassion [mercies], and the God of all comfort, who comforts us in all troubles [tribulations], so that we can comfort those in any trouble with the comfort we ourselves have received from [Papa] God.*

Comfort me, Papa.

We are comforted by Papa by being brought into His heart to rest. I ask You, Papa, to hold me until I am enabled to come to rest in Your heart.

Psalm 45:10-17 has become a very special passage for my life. Verse 13 says:

**Psalm 45:13 (AMP)**

> *The King's daughter in the inner part [of the palace] is all glorious; her clothing is inwrought with gold.*

I am glad to say that I am standing tall these days. One of the reasons is because of the following event.

Chapter 63

# Another Step in Discovering My True Identity

AFTER WE HAD MOVED to New York, I woke up one morning and heard the Holy Spirit say, "Alienation of affection." I thought, "What does that mean?" It made me think immediately of what some consider grounds for divorce. I sat this aside in my heart and pondered it for a while, waiting on the Holy Spirit for the understanding. It eventually came.

It started in the fall of 2010, my favorite season. The Lord chose some of my favorite people in my life to help me, my sisters in the Lord, my true family of God, and it started at the farmhouse.

We had decided to get together again, this time with a smaller, more intimate group, to pray, meet with the Lord, and just have some good fellowship. Two or three days into this wonderful time one of the sisters, Linda, received a word from the Holy Spirit that they were to have a celebration of my birthday, and the Father wanted this to be a surprise party for me.

It wasn't really my natural birthday, That was still months away. It was to specifically bless my birth — that day (and before) I was actually born.

Abba God told them what to get, how to decorate the house and table. He told them specific gifts to purchase and a lot more surprises. I was taken out of the house and distracted while the others got busy preparing the details of the surprise party. It was getting dark as Dorcas (the owner of the farm) and I drove into the driveway. It was dark inside, yet a dim light shone out of the windows. I could scarcely see movement inside and wondered what was going on. As we entered the house, I saw that these dear sisters (daughters of the King) had decorated the kitchen with small lights and candles. The table was set with every detail the Holy Spirit had instructed them.

I was shocked and couldn't believe my eyes. I asked "why" they would do this for me. They told me about the word and how Father God wanted to celebrate or bless my birth.

I was pleasantly surprised, yet somewhat confused still as to why? The answer to that question would begin to be answered a few months later. For now I just accepted this blessing. I enjoyed a beautiful cake and candles to blow out. This was healing for me because I could not ever remember any birthday parties when I was a child.

I opened my symbolic gifts from each sister. They all had

special meanings to me, like pomegranates and bells on the table. Each sister hand-picked gifts as the Holy Spirit directed her, which deeply touched me. They had been told to buy a journal and each wrote a birth blessing in it, which of course made me cry.

These were tears of healing (see Psalm 56:8), tears of joy, tears of deliverance, but mostly tears of love. I was deeply moved by their generosity and outpouring of love, but even more so by genuine display of affection for me.

Remember that phrase *alienation of affection* from earlier? Margriet came later and was told about the surprise party. She said the Lord had told her to be extravagant with her gifts, and she said she had so much fun choosing what to bring me. I was experiencing affection from Abba through these displays of love. I felt that I belonged.

To top it all off, the Holy Spirit set up a divine appointment for counseling. It was with a sweet older couple over in Canada (not a problem since I live on the border). They would help me gain a breakthrough with some anger issues in my life. The next week the Lord gave me the release to call them and go see them.

Chapter 64

# Back to the Future

AS I BEGAN TO wait on the Lord for His counsel on where to begin about my anger, He took us to the beginning — my beginning. In the beginning was the light. Light just so happened to be the meaning of my name — Elaine. I shared my history with the counselors, and we began to notice a common thread running throughout my whole life, especially in the early years. I had an identity crisis.

Your identity is you expressing who you were made to be. But the thief comes to steal, kill, and destroy. Everyone today is concerned or afraid of a new crime called identity theft. This occurs when someone steals or destroys who you are and pretends to be you. This is a very personal crime, as it wars against the person's spirit and soul.

Have you ever been a victim of this crime? I was. I suffered the theft of who I was and who I belonged to in Christ and Abba God.

But Jesus said:

**Luke 8:17**

*For nothing is hidden that shall not be disclosed, and nothing concealed that will not be known or brought out into the open.*

One of the things revealed to my counselor was that I had been conceived in lust, not love. I guess that should not have surprised me. I knew that my parents had been just teenagers, still in high school, when I was conceived. Nearing graduation, Dad had learned that he was to be a father, and it was a responsibility he had not bargained for. Mom was young and pretty, and they both thought they were in love. He was not really ready for a commitment of marriage, but before my birth, they did marry, and I was given his name.

The unwanted pregnancy put Mom in a difficult situation because she and her mother were both pregnant at the same time. Grandma was having what they called a change-of-life baby and was five months pregnant when I was conceived. So my mom was on her own with most of the pregnancy. (This, of course, is all hearsay from my mother, since I never knew my earthly father and, therefore, couldn't ask him for his side of the story.)

Since they were now married, Mom said she had been looking forward to my birth, but it turned out to be a very difficult delivery. For one thing, when she went into labor, she didn't have her mother there to help her. She was young, alone, and very frightened. At one point a nurse came in to check on her progress, and she said to Mom, "Oh my, this baby's head is very soft."

At that, Mom panicked and screamed, "I'm having a very bad contraction." In response to this, they gave her so much gas that she was knocked out, totally asleep.

It didn't take them long to discover that what the nurse had thought was a soft head was really my buttocks. Mom was having what they called a "full breech" presentation. I was coming out buttocks first, instead of head first. Now they had to work hard to try to turn me the other way since full breach is a very difficult and dangerous birth.

As hard as they tried, I seemed to be stuck, and it seems that my spirit took on that breech attitude that had been declared over me in the womb.

*Breech* can be defined as "the hinder part of anything," but *breach* (with a different spelling) can also mean "the breaking of a law, contract, or any other obligation, an opening or gap made by breaking, a rupture of friendly relations, and a disagreement to violate an agreement." My spirit became divided or broken in those moments. It discerned a violation of a law or contract, the law of love that was broken by my parents.

After I was born, Mom, being young and permissive, didn't have the discipline or self-control needed to stay home and nurture me properly. She preferred to go out dancing with other men, betraying my father in the process.

On top of all this, while I was still in the womb, my human spirit had begun to blame myself for the pain suffered by my parents. I felt guilty. If not for me, if not for my birth, they would have been just fine. "My birth was a terrible mistake," I kept thinking, and "my conception should never have happened. All the wrong that followed was all my fault."

According to an article by Kathy Oates posted on The Elijah List, "Our spirit knows what has happened to us from conception to this very day:

**Proverbs 14:19**

*Each heart knows its own bitterness,*
*and no one else can share its joy.*

"Your spirit knows the real truth about everything that has occurred in your life, and mine, and, of course Abba God knows the real truth too."

**Proverbs 20:27**

*The lamp of the Lord searches the spirit of a man,*
*it searches out his inmost being.*

"Your innermost being has registered everything that has ever happened to you and me. Your spirit knows every thought you have ever had. Even in the womb, your spirit records your life." [11]

A spirit of illegitimacy now accused me in my human spirit or heart, that I didn't have a right to exist. I was illegal.

One of the gifts I received at my surprise birthday party was from the Father. He had someone buy me a gold heart-shaped locket. Inside it said "You are Mine!" When I read that, it hit me very hard deep in my spirit. Mentally, of course, I knew this truth, yet deep in my spirit, because it had been wounded by the spirit of illegitimacy, I couldn't feel that affection. I never felt like I truly belonged. I felt lost inside.

This was my heartcry:

**Psalm 86:11-12 (MSG)**
> *Put me together, one heart and mind,*
> *then, undivided, I'll worship in joyful fear.*

I was still that little girl playing the TV game *I've Got A Secret,* looking for the authentic Elaine to stand up and be recognized. By the mercy and grace of my heavenly Father, who knew the real secret, He was beginning to reveal it to me by the Spirit.

Chapter 65

# "Do You Promise To Tell?"

ONE NIGHT I HAD a dream, an encounter with the Lord Jesus, and He began to sing in my ear an old Beatles' song. It said, "Do you want to know a secret?" The original words had been "Do you promise *not* to tell," but He changed some of the words for it to say, "Do you promise to tell? Let me whisper in your ear. Come closer, closer, closer." Over and over, for weeks, He began to reveal the secret mystery of my identity. Oh, hallelujah, I am His!

**Psalm 51:6**
> *Surely you desire truth in the inner parts;*
> *you teach me wisdom in the inmost [hidden] place.*

According to John and Paula Sanford, in their book, *Healing the Wounded Spirit*, after conception, my personal spirit went to sleep. "The Bible calls this a slumbering spirit. It is when your own spirit is not awake, and it is not alert and functioning." [12]

Before I explain this further, let me say that this is not to make excuses for myself or others like me. It is, rather, to bring understanding to us of the need to love people who suffer in this way and help them heal. It is to set them free.

It has been revealed to the Sanfords that there are two kinds of slumbering spirits. There are those who have never been drawn to life who, early in infancy, have fallen asleep and can no longer function. This was my case. Secondly, there are those who did receive parental nurture and so were awake and functioning spiritually, but turned away from worship services, prayer, and affection until their spirits fell asleep. In both cases, the heart has usually hardened as well (see Hebrews 3:8 and 15).

The Sanfords go on to say it is only in the areas of relationship to God, man, nature or their own being (who am I?) that these sleepers cannot function in their spirits. They can share in emotion, weeping over the lost, and about their own sins through remorse, but are not able to either commune with Jesus or share in His sufferings as Paul related in Philippians 3:10.

I remained asleep until, by the mercy and grace of Yahweh, I received the baptism of the Holy Spirit (as described in an earlier chapter).

Now let us go back to the place we left off at the surprise birthday party. Remember the Holy Spirit had spoken to me the words *alienation of affection*. Even though, at this time in my life, my spirit has been awakened, it woke up to a messy room (my soul). I was awake and excited to be alive, but as I looked around my heart, I found how many messes my soul had made.

The Sanfords write, "We want to make it very clear that if our parents fail to give nurture, we are set in patterns of sin by our sinful responses. We can never be said to be irresponsible. We will be held accountable for our responses to those people who wounded us, but we are not accountable for the wound (mess) themselves. The remedy for sinful response is forgiveness. The remedy for wounds is healing. No nurture is as vitally important to the human spirit as affection." [13]

My mother, being unprepared in so many ways, was unable to provide the affection a newborn needed. Thus, the alienation of affection began. I personally believe that the breech birth somehow brought with it this alienation of my spirit to my parents.

I need to clarify why I am using the two words, *breach* and *breech*, interchangeably. I am aware of the two separate meanings, but our Lord loves to do a play on words to prophetically speak to us. The baby in the womb heard and felt the word used by the nurse (*breach*), but was also saturated with fear. Again the definition of *breech* is "the hinder part of anything," yet this word sounds the same as *breach,* "the breaking of a law, contract or any obligation, an opening or gap."

A *breach of promise* is "a failure to keep one's promise, especially to marry." There appeared to be an opening or gap of affection toward me on the part of my parents.

Threads of Gold

The definition of *affection* is "the state of having feelings, touched, or excited." *Attachment, fondness, tenderness,* and *love* are all synonymous with *affection.* Antonyms for this are *enmity, hostile, indifference,* and *aversion.* So my mother and father, who were to be the primary nurturers or life givers to me, failed to do it, and starvation of affection began.

"Without touch, the human spirit starves. With touch, the spirit expands, and a person learns who and what their identity is, relishes life, cherishes others, and becomes strong. Without touch and affection, the spirit shrivels and withdraws inside and closes its eyes." [14]

This is what had happened to me.

Chapter 66

# Sleeping Beauty

**Ephesians 6:4**

*Fathers, do not exasperate your children; instead, bring them up in the training and instruction of the Lord.*

"FATHERS ARE EXPECTED TO be the primary person in the raising of children. The father is the one who is designed by God to call the spirit forth with courage and to be. The mother is to balance, support, and encourage that process. 'To be or not to be that is the question.'"[15] Neither my father nor mother were around.

Mom wasn't physically able to breast feed me, so I was fed by anyone with a propped bottle. It was upon finding me in a very sad condition one day that my father decided that enough was enough. There had been some infidelity on my mother's part, so he made up his mind to leave us and divorce her.

After returning home from work at night, he would find me still in my crib. My soiled diapers had not been changed all day. He also found me with curdled milk in my bottle numerous times. In time, I became so weak and sick with pneumonia that I was placed in an iron lung. (I was told this by aunts, uncles, and my grandmother, not by my parents.)

Eventually, my father made arrangements for me to be taken care of by my mother's older sister in New Orleans and took me there by train, unbeknownst to my mother. She was frantic when she returned home to find me missing. My father had asked Grandma to take me, but she had a six-month-old baby of her own to care for. She knew, however, where to send me.

Grandma calmed Mom down by telling her I was safe with her sister. This ended up being a thirteen-year stay. Again the Sanfords say, "To the degree of the parents' failure, especially the father, children's spirits fall asleep." [16] Although I was very young, my spirit recorded all of this. The real me went to sleep. This is why, at the tender age of eight or nine, watching that TV show *I've Got A Secret* enthralled me. Deep inside was a secret, a truth.

"A tremendous fallacy in the western way of thinking is to equate intellectual assent to knowing the truth. Christianity then becomes a mental cerebral experience. But knowing in your mind does not mean you know it is the truth. The word *know* in scripture indicates intimacy. If I have intimacy with or know the truth, the truth will set me free. And the Truth, all the Truth is a person — Jesus. Anything contradictory to Jesus is a lie." [17]

Chapter 67

# The Truth, the Whole Truth and Nothing but the Truth

**John 8:32 (KJV)**
*And ye shall know the truth, and the truth shall make you free.*

"THE TRUTH, THE WHOLE truth, and nothing but the truth." I kept hearing this statement over and over in my spirit. It is what we hear people say when they are sworn to testify in court. They place their hand on the Bible and say this: "I swear to tell the truth, the whole truth and nothing but the truth, so help me God." If they are asked the question, they respond: "I do."

"So, help me, God," I prayed, "help me to understand why You are saying this phrase to me. There must be a distinction between truths or why would it be necessary to state it three ways?" In time, this is what the Holy Spirit, the Spirit of Truth, showed me:

THE TRUTH: is my side of the story, how I remembered (or not) things in my life. I would relate the details as the truth, as best I could.

THE WHOLE TRUTH: is getting other people's point of view on the same story, the way they remember the details of having lived it.

NOTHING BUT THE TRUTH: is when He who is the Truth comes and reveals nothing but the truth to you, and knowing intimately the Truth sets you free. Jesus is the way, the Truth, and nothing but the Truth!

The truth, as I saw it, was what I have already discussed concerning my breach birth. But here is another point of view, or what I have defined as "the whole truth":

After my natural father took me away, provisions were made, unbeknownst to my mother, that he would take me by train to my aunt and uncle in New Orleans. Little did I know that this would be the last time I would see him. My entire life I held him in high esteem for this one reason: He went with me and provided a safe place for me to live. That was all I knew about the man. (This was all secondhand knowledge that came through relatives, as I was only a little over a year old when it happened and so I had no memory of it at all.) This one act of kindness, my father's last one toward me, allowed my heart to cherish his memory. It also allowed my heart that was wounded within me through abandonment to receive my heavenly Father's love later, much later.

His Word says of Him:

**Hosea 14:3**

*In you the fatherless find compassion.*

**Psalm 10:14**

*You are the helper of the fatherless.*

**Psalm 109:21-22**

*But you, O Sovereign Lord, deal well with me for your name's sake;*
*out of the goodness of your love, deliver me.*
*For I am poor and needy, and my heart is wounded within me.*

Jesus said:

**John 14:18**

*I will not leave you as orphans; I will come to you.*

Where are Your true Shepherds, Papa?

Chapter 68

# A True Shepherd

I WAS WEARING MY gold heart locket around my neck. I would feel it with my fingers and occasionally open it. I would read what it said inside "You are Mine." Since it is the father's role to call his children's spirit forth with courage and to be, this was beginning to happen for me, not through my earthly father, but through my heavenly Papa God.

The counselor I was led to consult was Bob Bayles. I called to make an appointment with him and his wife for prayer counseling. His voice was soft, and tender, comforting me. I felt safe talking to him, *"I am the God of all comfort,"* I heard in my spirit.

**2 Corinthians 1:2-4 (AMP)**

*Grace (favor and spiritual blessings) to you and [heart] peace from God our Father and the Lord Jesus Christ (the Messiah, the Anointed One). Blessed be the God and Father of our Lord Jesus Christ, the Father of sympathy (pity and mercy) and the God (Who is the*

*Source) of every comfort (consolation and encourage-
ment), who comforts (consoles and encourages) us in
every trouble (calamity and affliction) so that we may
also be able to comfort those who are in any kind of
trouble with which we ourselves are comforted (consoled
and encouraged) by God.*

**Isaiah 40:1-2 (AMP)**

*Comfort, comfort My people says your God. Speak
tenderly to the heart of Jerusalem, and cry to her that
her time of service and her warfare are ended, that [her
punishment is accepted and] her iniquity is pardoned,
that she has received [punishment] from the Lord's hand
double for all her sins.*

Here on the phone was a shepherd who was speaking tenderly
to me, and my spirit was at peace. My soul was at rest. I could
trust this true shepherd.

We met in their home in Ontario. It is a lovely home with
plenty of flowers and a warm inviting atmosphere. More importantly, God was there. I could sense His presence.

I was invited into the living room to sit, and Shelley, Bob's
wife and co-laborer, offered me something to drink. She is, well,
like a mother — caring and welcoming, with a beautiful smile.
They are both engaging. I felt good in their living room, rather
than in some stuffy office with a minister looking down at me
from over his big desk.

Even as I write these words on paper, my eyes are full of hot tears. They are healing tears. This man and woman made me feel like I was wanted, invited, and welcomed. The whole experience was scary for me, but it was also wonderful!

I was in expectation mode, as I shared with these lovely people why I was there. I said I had a lot of pain, and was not yet able to release it. I said, "It is like I have a guard-dog guarding my heart full of pain, and he won't allow it to flow out." The name of this watch dog was anger. I thought if I could somehow get rid of the anger, the dog would go away, and I could be set free of the pain. We prayed together, the three of us, and then the journey began.

Paul Cox has written, "Through Christ's shed blood on the cross, we have the provision, as we accept that sacrifice, to return to the ancient paths."

**Jeremiah 6:16 (KJV)**
> *Thus saith the Lord, Stand ye in the ways, and see, and ask for the old [ancient] paths where is the good way, and walk therein, and ye shall find rest for your souls.*

"We must take back the land, our birthright, given away to the enemy. We must come against the strongholds in the land (of our hearts), our inheritance, and take back what the enemy has stolen. Return to the ancient pathways." [18]

Chapter 69

# Nothing But the Truth Arrives

AS WE WAITED SILENTLY, after praying and asking the Holy Spirit where to start, He showed us the old path. I was conceived out of lust and not love. At the time of conception, I believe the Holy Spirit revealed, a generational spirit had been inserted into my life from my family line. It was a spirit of illegitimacy. We continued praying.

My human spirit, after conception, became confused and stuck. I was stuck in the form of not knowing my identity (who am I?). Because of being conceived in an act of lust and not love, this brought confusion.

**John 8:44**

> *You belong to your father, the devil, and you want to carry out your father's desire. He was a murderer from the beginning, not holding to truth, for there is no truth in him. When he lies, he speaks his native language, for he is a liar and the father of lies.*

Henry Malone has written, "The iniquities of the fathers have been passed on to us, their children, and often we do not even recognize these behaviors and thoughts for what they are. Anger, inferiority, anxiety, lust, jealousy, infirmities, control, pride, and haughtiness have all been inherited from those who walked before us, beginning with Adam. We must reclaim our body, soul, and spirit from the dark forces that have controlled us (even parents). We must drive out the dark shadows in order to walk in the pure light that Jesus provided for us by His birth, death, and resurrection." [19] This is done by grace.

My first memories at conception were lies:

> *This should not have happened.*
> *I am a mistake.*
> *I am the one responsible and am guilty, therefore, of this happening.*

These were all lies. This is exactly what even small children do when they discover their parents are getting a divorce. They blame themselves. They feel guilty and responsible, when none of it is their doing.

In prayer, we asked the Lord Jesus to come and reveal the "whole truth and nothing but the truth."

**John 14:6**
> *Jesus answered, "I am the way and the truth and the life. No one comes to the Father except through me.*

The Lord Jesus came to me in that memory and revealed the source of what the false father (the father of lies) had spoken to me. Jesus spoke to my human spirit that what Satan had told me was indeed a lie, no truth was in it, nor was I guilty. Most of my life I had manifested anger because I had felt injustice and a lot of shame. This was because I had agreed with the father of lies that my birth was unjust and should never have happened.

Because of feeling illegal, due to a lying spirit of illegitimacy, I felt I had no voice or right to be heard. How could I ever get justice? In what court? Where was my advocate? Why did I always feel that I didn't belong? I was scared, lost, and alone. I heard the heavenly Father God say to me what I now knew to be the whole truth — "Justice is Mine!"

Because of the wounding in my spirit from rejection and abandonment, I blamed Abba God for allowing it to occur. I was angry at Him. True to form, the father of lies accused Father God, my true Father, of having caused the breach in our relationship. Therefore, I didn't know my true identity. The truth is that He had always been with me and would never leave me nor forsake me.

It was because of agreeing with the liar, that anger and confusion were in my heart, and I blamed Abba God. I belonged to Him. Why didn't I know this as truth?

I repented (changed my mind toward my heavenly Father) and turned from believing the falsehood or lie about

Papa God. I hadn't been able to see this lie to repent of it until the Lord Jesus came and showed me the way out, the truth (that set me free) and the life (out of death, slumber) and brought me to the Father (see John 14:6). I was making progress.

Chapter 70

# *Another Lie Revealed*

ANOTHER LIE THAT WAS revealed during prayer ministry was that I was guilty of my mother having the breech birth. She became filled with a spirit of fear upon hearing the nurse's voice say to her, "Oh, this baby's head is very soft." Her fear filled me also. She was given too much gas (a procedure common in the 1940s) and was knocked out. So, of course, she and I didn't bond upon my birth, because we were both too groggy, sleepy from the gas. My human spirit in fear went to sleep. Thus the slumbering spirit developed. (This is all by divine revelation to me from the Holy Spirit.)

I repented for blaming Abba God for this injustice. I then forgave my young parents for conceiving me in lust, which is betrayal. I then released many tears and anguish of soul, the pain, and the grief from the truth that I was violated and not conceived in love.

Then the Lord Jesus said to me, "You are not guilty." The gavel in His court of mercy and forgiveness was heard loudly.

Finally, I did have an Advocate, a voice on my behalf. His voice silences all others. I released the pain and the grief from guilt and shame. I took responsibility and repented for all the bad judgments of the little girl just conceived for allowing darkness in (by agreeing with it), and I commanded the spirit of confusion to go in Jesus name.

Let there be light. Again, that just happens to be what my name means: Elaine "light, understanding, illumination and brilliance." And, again, there is no such word as *coincidence* in the Hebrew language. My Abba had named me, and He watches over His Word to perform it.

So many times, throughout my life, I would accuse God of not watching over His word in me. If my name means light, where was light for me? I was given plenty (prophetically) for others. Here again, was the spirit of confusion working to keep the breech (breach) between Papa God and me. This lie usually manifested in my life through unfulfilled expectations. I would expect Him to come and be there for others but not for me.

One day, while still living in Kansas City, I had heard the Holy Spirit say to me in my car, "You need to let Me bless your expectations." I had cursed them by speaking lies over my life in this area. Yet (praise the Lord for the yet times in my life), the one redeeming memory that gave me hope was my natural dad taking me to a safe place to live. I intuitively knew that my Papa God would also take me to a safe place when I would finally allow Him, through forgiveness, to do it. Now I allowed Him this, by being willing to go through the pain of allowing the Holy Spirit to get rid of the guard dog in my heart. I allowed Him, by being willing to allow the light to shine in the dark places and reveal the lies. I allowed Him to show me the Truth, and now I'm telling you about it.

When the truth comes, it does set you free instantly, immediately, and indeed forever — without striving. The lies are gone by God's great grace. He takes them away, then He not only takes you to a safe place; He is the safe place. I was in His heart all along. He is my Refuge.

Chapter 71

# *Reminded of a Vision*

I WAS REMINDED OF a vision I'd had years earlier. In the vision, or picture, I saw an old-fashioned nursery in a hospital with rows and rows of baby bassinets (as were used years ago in hospitals). I saw Papa God come into the nursery, come over to my crib, and look at me. He smiled and placed an ID bracelet on my tiny wrist that said: "Daddy's Girl." He then said, "You belong to Me."

I was helpless and unable to perform anything for Him, just to be. His is a gift of grace.

At the time I had this vision, it impacted me deeply, yet (there is that word again) a large part of me, my human spirit had to receive this by faith. Now after repenting and receiving forgiveness for my part, I could feel the belonging of my Father God and His family. Arthur Burke says, "It is knowing the Father that imparts in us the belonging, knowing Jesus imparts worth, and knowing the Holy Spirit value. We need all three for our full identity." [20] I was beginning to know and feel like I was "Daddy's Girl."

I believe that, way back then, He gave me a permanent ID bracelet, and my identity was sure in Him.

**Psalm 89:14**

> *Righteousness and justice are the foundations of your throne;*
> *love and faithfulness go before you.*

I couldn't experience the glory of the Lord flowing over me and through me fully until I released from my human spirit resentments and judgments toward my parents, even those I was unaware of.

Jesus said:

**Matthew 7:16 (AMP)**

> *You will fully recognize them by their fruits.*

Bitter-root judgments and sins of resentment that were made by faith were experienced (no matter how young). The psalmist said:

**Psalm 139:23-24**

> *Search me, O God, and know my heart;*
> *test me and know my anxious thoughts,*
> *See if there is any offensive way in me,*
> *and lead me in the way everlasting.*

During this prayer ministry time, I released any resentment or unforgiveness toward myself about this particular issue, and I received the sentence of the Righteous Judge: "not guilty" and "forgiven." I received His blood washing in Jesus for me.

**Psalm 35:4**

> *May those who seek my life*
> *be disgraced and put to shame;*
> *may those who plot my ruin*
> *be turned back in dismay.*

Everything the enemy meant for evil in my life Abba God had now redeemed for good (see Genesis 50:20).

Chapter 72

# A Father's and Mother's Blessing

TO CONCLUDE OUR TIME together, Bob and Shelley placed their hands on me and proclaimed a father and mother's blessing over me. They asked the Lord Jesus to awaken and draw my spirit forth with liveliness and enthusiasm and also asked to stop all death wishes, bitter-root judgments, and expectancies that had resulted from being starved for affection.

I'm sure those were not the very words used, but they do represent the spirit of the ministry. The reason I don't have the exact words is that, although Shelley is a wonderful scribe during prayer counseling, she had laid aside her writing to be able to be a part of the hands-on blessing. We had discussed this and were all on the same page. I had a need for human touch through which God's Spirit would do the work. The Lord supplied love, which I missed in infancy via my parents. We asked the Holy Spirit to minister to the inner child.

The most critical part of healing for slumbering spirits, as I was delivered from, is that the condition requires the Church to be community. It is not enough for ex-slumberers like me to have what the church usually calls "Christian fellowship." I needed more, and others do too. We need some part of the true Body of Christ to be there as family, like the Bayles were doing in prayer, to provide what my natural family was unable to give me.

This is why a small, intimate group appealed to me, because it supplied what I needed so badly. Just looking at the back of the heads of someone on Sunday mornings was not enough to resurrect me. Church suppers, pastoral calls, church meetings and study groups would not get the desired results. These were too detached, distant, cold, and unengaged at deep heart levels. These do meet a need, but only as background, not as the whole. I desperately needed (and so do others with slumbering spirits) to be re-parented by mothers and fathers in Christ.

Do you now understand with more clarity why we have a cry in the Kingdom for mothers and fathers, not just teachers? In writing to the Galatians, Paul said it best:

**Galatians 4:9**

> *I am again in the pains of childbirth until Christ is formed in you.*

## A Father's and Mother's Blessing

This is exactly what Bob and Shelley, as well as many other faithful friends, were accomplishing in the Spirit with me.

Chapter 73

# A Powerful Prayer

I FOUND ON THE Internet a prayer written by Paul Cox called to release the abundant life. [21] It is quite lengthy, but I urge you to go to his website and take a look at it for yourself. It was one more tool given to me to change my thinking, and I believe it will help you too.

Here is the ending of my personal prayer:

> I claim my spiritual birthright of being con-
> ceived in love, of being given the Spirit of
> Yahweh, who reveals wisdom to me, and of
> being given spiritual eyes in my heart to see
> the riches of His glorious inheritance. I claim
> that I am being formed in the image of His
> glorious Son Jesus. I reject the seed of Satan,
> and I reject my former position as a child of
> the father of lies and murderer.

I ask You, Abba Father, to close the eyes that were opened when Adam and Eve partook of the tree of the knowledge of good and evil. I declare that my Redeemer lives, and while I am yet alive, I will see Abba God for myself with my own eyes.

I declare that my hope is in You, my Redeemer. I ask You now to restore the ancient pathways to me and shine Your Light on me so I can see You with my own eyes. I ask You to restore my stolen birthright back to me, my glory and my crown.

Father, I thank You that before You formed me in my mother's womb, You predetermined my birthright, the path of glory I should walk in. Lord, would You cause me to dwell in the secret place of the Most High.

I declare that my birthright is to walk with Abba Father in the garden where I hear His voice, and enjoy intimate fellowship with Him. I believe that Jesus Christ, my Lord, appropriated this intimacy for me when He ripped the veil in the Holy of Holies.

Lord, I repent for my generational line, that we tried to earn by works that which you had given freely by grace. Lord, please now usher me into that place of rest and perfect peace.

Now, here is a secret that I learned:

**Matthew 10:26-27**

> *Do not be afraid of them. There is nothing con-*
> *cealed that will not be disclosed, or hidden that*
> *will not be made known. What I tell you in the*
> *dark speak in the daylight; what is whispered in*
> *your ear, proclaim from the roofs.*

**Matthew 5:14-16**

> *You are the light of the world. A city on a hill*
> *cannot be hidden. Neither do people light and put*
> *it under a bowl. Instead, they put it on its stand,*
> *and it gives light to everyone in the house. In the*
> *same way, let your light shine before men, that they*
> *may see your good deeds and praise your Father in*
> *heaven.*

I pray this is what I have done, to His glory. What had begun for me as a journey of discovery lasted over a decade. It ended when I finally got understanding of the experience of those long-lost years. Paul wrote:

**Romans 11:36, AMP**

> *For from Him and through Him and to Him are*
> *all things. (For all things originate with Him and*
> *come from Him; all things live through Him, and*

*all things center in and tend to consummate and to end in Him.) To Him be glory forever! Amen (so be it).*

Amen!

Chapter 74

# *The Continued Blessing of the Farmhouse*

WHEN I MET DORCAS, I could not be sure what God was doing. We met in her place, and since then there have been glorious Kingdom gatherings in that place. I feel truly honored and humbled to have this family in my life. We have all been blessed in so many ways by their obedience.

This book revolves around the Emerging Bride Gathering that took place at that very farmhouse. All you have read about the Jewish Wedding ceremonies, the *chuppah,* and glorious events that touched so many people were at this place. There angels come and meet with us (as they do with whoever comes there). There is an open heaven over that place because of the intercession and dedication of those who own it to those who visit.

It was from this place that the Bridal Wave broke out and began to expand to all parts of the United States —

north, south, east, and west — and to the nearby nations and beyond. Now that call has been heard and answered to "Come over here and help us." I said "yes" and those who were scattered abroad also say "yes" to their call.

Chapter 75

# My Joy in Working with the Canadians

IT WAS 2012 WHEN I heard the cry to come over and help the brothers and sisters of Ontario, Canada, and I am so blessed to be associated with them. Now, over the past fourteen years that I have been living up here in Upstate New York, I have stitched across the borders of these two nations many times.

The Canadian people humble me because they are so hungry for more of God. They have rolled out a red carpet for me to come, release the revelation, and help them experience the Bridegroom relationship for themselves.

These people were not dead, but had only been sleeping, like *Talitha cumi*. We cry to them, "Arise, Canada, this is your time to shine with the glory of the Lord upon you. This is the time for us, as two neighboring nations, to bring healing to the breaches."

## My Joy in Working with the Canadians

It is not a coincidence that the Canadian flag has a maple leaf on it. As I have mentioned several times, no such word as coincidence exists in Hebrew. That maple leaf stands for the healing of the nations. The stitching has begun, and the mending has started in Yeshua's Holy name.

Thank you, my sisters and friends, for bringing healing to this friend and to America. I thank our Abba for allowing us to share borders of peace together. I thank You, Father, for building bridges of hope between us, as neighbors and as family in Messiah. I thank You, Abba, that we are waking up as Your Bride. Yeshua, as the Desire of the Nations, has come to kiss His beauty.

In the book entitled *The Chronicles of Narnia,* after Aslan is resurrected from the dead, he tells the young ladies to climb upon his back and cover their ears. They climb upon him, and he roars.

The people he goes to are those the wicked witch has put to sleep. He goes up to each person and breathes on them, and they are no longer frozen or asleep. His breath wakes them up. Oh, Lord, come as the Lion now and roar over Your defeated enemy, Death/Slumber/Apathy/Indifference. Come, Lord Jesus, and breathe on us. Your Bride is waking up.

The Spirit and the Bride agree, and we say, "Come." We are not dead. We have just been sleeping, but now we are waking up to Your call to rule and reign with You, King Yeshua, our Messiah.

Amen!

Dear Readers,

I have not attempted to recall my whole life from beginning to end. I simply followed the ebb and flow of the Holy Spirit, as He led me. Just like the pattern on a magnificent wedding dress, His leading can follow exact lines and then change randomly into a whole new pattern or design. He is the Master Designer, not me.

Elaine Perry

*Appendices*

# Notes from the Emerging Bride Gathering
## (July 10-11, 2010)

During the Emerging Bride Gathering, Mary Ellen took the following notes:

Gloria heard angels singing, "He reigns! He reigns! He Reigns!" over and over, all night long, after our individual experience with Him in the *chuppah*. She said, "There was a break in the spirit after all we did in the *chuppah*. White glory came over the land in waves. About 1:00 AM in the morning Linda Kahler saw the white glory waves and spent some time validating that it wasn't fog or a tree line or any other such natural thing.

Gloria knew that the angels watched each of us in the *chuppah*. They sang our names — each one over and over: Elaine ... Linda ... Chelsea ... Gloria ... Jen ... Marilyn ... Dorcas ... Cindy ... Leanne ... Allison ... Linda ... Carmen ... Donna ... Mary Ellen ... Stevie ... Mindy ... Margriet ... Tish.

The angels rejoiced over us, and Gloria sensed their non-stop activity all night, as they continued to sing and declare: "He reigns! He reigns! He reigns over this land, over this region, over the places where we are going."

The angels saw us go into the *chuppah* and come out. Father was pleased, and the angels gave Him glory all night to bless the Father to see His emerging Bride."

**Habakkuk 2:2 (NKJV)**
> *Then the Lord answered me and said:*
>
> *"Write the vision*
> *And make it plain on tablets,*
> *That he may run who reads it.*

In Gloria and Linda came a double witness, a matter decided by God. Really.

**Habakkuk 2:1 (NKJV)**
> *I will stand my watch*
> *And set myself on the rampart,*
> *And watch to see what He will say to me.*

Such a light is upon this land. It is a type of ark, shelter, lighthouse, refuge, and healing station in the name of Jesus. It is a sanctuary for the presence of the Lord, a place for Him to dwell and reign.

Thus saith the Lord on this day, July 11 (the number of the prophets), 2010: "Come to the banqueting table, come and dine. Come to the feeding station. This is a Red Cross station for the sick in spirit, soul, and body. It is a triage. It is a place of cleansing, receiving ministry, and then going out in strength."

Dorcas heard the sound of clapping and snapping fingers, and an angel woke her up. She knew she had to get dressed and go downstairs. Gloria and Linda were sharing their testimonies.

Elaine arrived, also having been awakened and told to get to the farm. She shared the following: She heard the Lord ask her to stay in the *chuppah*, just after it was set up. She knew He was waiting for her and for each of us. His angels were there recording it. Zephaniah 3:17 came to mind with the reports of all-night singing:

**Zephaniah 3:17 (NKJV)**
> *The LORD your God in your midst,*
> *The Mighty One will save;*
> *He will rejoice over you with gladness,*
> *He will quiet you with His love,*
> *He will rejoice over you with singing.*

She also shared a recent revelation of "My yoke is easy and my burden is light." The "easy yoke" means to be in His presence, His glory, where everything flows with ease. The "light" burden is His revelatory word that brings understanding, direction, and clarification. She was hearing, "Baa, Baa, Black Sheep, have you any wool?" She believes those coming to the farm will be those suffering from rejection by other sheep and/or those who are wounded or weary and need healing and refreshing. God made our eyes single and full of light as we emerged as His Bride.

Gloria said that she believes the continuous singing and presence of the angels reflect the continuous renewing of His covenant with us and perpetual blessing. All rights have been conferred and all promises secured to us and those who come here.

Linda Vaughan said that before coming to New York she saw Elaine as a five-star general. She is the commander-in-chief in God. Each of us in the Emerging Bride is a general, but Elaine is our chief commander in God. She gets the download from the Father and releases it to us. He brought the generals together and has assigned this time.

Hearing "Light and Glory."

**Isaiah 60:1-3 (NKJV)**

> *Arise, shine;*
> *For your light has come!*
> *And the glory of the LORD is risen upon you.*
> *For behold, the darkness shall cover the earth,*
> *And deep darkness the people;*
> *But the LORD will arise over you,*

*And His glory will be seen upon you.*
*The Gentiles shall come to your light,*
*And kings to the brightness of your rising.*

What happened in the *chuppah* last night is that each of us emerged as generals in the Lord's army. From here the light of the Bride will go out over the world. The Lord told Linda before coming, "New York is the gateway to Israel." We've carried it and birthed it here. The bridal wave has begun. This is the whiteout, the Bride going out as God leads.

God told Linda to call the Bride to unity and holiness, but she didn't know how to do that. She heard the *shofars* calling us into unity. We are to unite with those who hear the call, love them, give of ourselves to them, and receive love from them.

We must forsake compromise, break every agreement with Satan, renounce everything and every time we've agreed with him — known and unknown. We must align ourselves with the Lord and His covenant, resist Satan and every evil thing.

Elaine heard that (Yahweh) God is watching over Israel, the Land of Israel and spiritual Israel.

**Psalm 121:4 (NKJV)**
*Behold, He who keeps Israel*
*Shall neither slumber nor sleep.*

Gloria heard: "Hephzibah."

**Isaiah 62:4 (NKJV)**

> *You shall no longer be termed Forsaken,*
> *Nor shall your land any more be termed Desolate;*
> *But you shall be called Hephzibah, and your land*
> *Beulah;*
> *For the LORD delights in you,*
> *And your land shall be married.*

The Lord is enlarging our territory and extending our boundaries. Everyone's capacity for the Lord has increased. He has enlarged territory in each of us for more of Him, and therefore, our spirit influence has changed.

We must lie down with Jesus and get up with the Father.

Gloria told Allison that because she was the one who broke the seals on the oils last night, she will also break the seals of many more anointings and will leak as she walks in the paths the Lord has chosen for her. God is going to fill you, Allison, with new oil and give you a master key of love.

A crown and scepter were given to Elaine and Gloria. When we came out of the *chuppah,* there were formations in the clouds resembling a crown, a scepter, and a huge winged angel in flight. I wished I'd had my camera handy. All of us saw these things clearly in the sky. It was amazing.

Then we all sang the song:

> *You shall go out with joy and be led forth with peace.*
> *The mountains and the hills will break forth before you.*

*There'll be shouts of joy and all the trees of the field
will clap, will clap their hands.
And all the trees of the field will clap their hands.
The trees of the field will clap their hands
The trees of the field will clap their hands
And you'll go out with joy.*

**Isaiah 55:12 (NKJV)**

*"For you shall go out with joy,
And be led out with peace;
The mountains and the hills
Shall break forth into singing before you,
And all the trees of the field shall clap their hands.*

## Some Words Shared Around the Table Before Leaving

We are all to go forth shaking the keys of the Kingdom and telling the enemy, "You are trespassing!" We are carrying the keys of the Kingdom of Heaven now.

Every person in the Kingdom has great value. God is shaking things up, and we need to be taking territory for the Kingdom instead of trying to get comfortable.

We need to be excited about who we are in the Lord. If you don't know who you are, you can't stand in the authority you have. We need to let our party out and trump their party. We are being purged with Holy Ghost Ex Lax to live out the holiness of God and God's movement. When it's darkest, we must remember that the Deliverer has already been birthed. God can extract the enemy from your life just as easily as He took Israel out of Egypt. Every time there is a new call on your life, there is another trip to the desert.

Then we sang the song: My Deliverer Is Coming.

Seed carriers grow harvest. We cannot abandon the crop until it is harvested. We must lay claim and stand our ground. Declare, "This valley is mine!

"We are the Kingdom of God, and we need to start living it. We need to take back our land of America. This is a spiritual revolution, and it is the only solution. We must take a stand. We must stand guard.

"While I was in the *chuppah,* the Lord said to me, 'The nations are yours, Beloved. I will put them in your mouth and in your heart and carry you there on eagle's wings.' I believe this word is for all of us.

"The Spirit and the Bride say, Come!" Jesus is the Spirit of prophecy. Selah!"

— **Mary Ellen**

# Testimonies From the Emerging Bride Gathering

Here are some of the testimonies of those who attended the Emerging Bride Gathering:

### Testimony #1

In the winter of 2008-09, I reconnected with Elaine by phone after a year or more without conversation, and she told me about the conference she was planning in New York. While my heart was more than anxious to be a part, I never dreamed I'd actually attend.

Then, in the spring of 2009, my friend Linda in Missouri met Elaine through Facebook. They had a similar conversation about the conference, and Linda, too, wanted to attend. Before long, all three of us joined by conference call and prayed for an opening to go.

Slowly and miraculously the plans unfolded, and

on June 30 Linda and I flew to New York and then drove five hours to Ogdensburg. What transpired over those next two weeks is still bearing fruit today. The accommodations were picturesque and far beyond our expectations. The home was warm, comfortable, and inviting. There was an immediate sense of peace and the presence of Holy Spirit.

When the conference began I was amazed and blessed by the diversity and the beauty of the women, professional business, and government women, homemakers, newly married and singles, women of every age range, and yet we shared a common love for the Lord and each other. In no time at all, we were sharing our hearts in worship and conversation, our hands in food preparation and ministry, and our time blessing each other and the Lord.

I watched the transformation of each one, as burdens and insecurities fell away, and beautiful confident brides emerged. We each valued the time to share with sisters who spoke our language and brought understanding to the issues in life we were facing. I gained a greater appreciation for my own and others' giftings. The teachings, the music, the oils, and the many little extras made each of us feel loved and valued, important to the King and to the Kingdom. I personally came home with a greater confidence to exercise my authority as His Bride and reclaim my home area for the King through prayer, declaration, and ministry. I came home with tools, encouragement, and a better sense of direction.

Thank you again to each one that made this conference one I will never forget and one I hope to repeat soon and bring others to benefit as I did.

— *Mary Ellen*

### *Testimony #2*

Royalty in our Savior, we overcome by becoming a part of the Bride of Christ. I felt special to the Lord as I left the New York gathering. An intimacy developed that allows me to feel more of His great grace and love. The closeness with the ladies was also a delight to me.

I was going through a rough time with our son at the time, and the experience was such a refreshing for me. Thank you for the wonderful experience. The remembrance brings such comfort to me.

— *Carmen Miller*

### *Testimony #3*

What an amazing time it was and an amazing ride it has been. I was so blessed to be with each one of you. Only our heavenly Father can orchestrate such a gathering.

Emerging Bride: *to emerge*, "to move out of or away from something to come into view."

This process of becoming the Bride of Christ is a continual moving forward, moving out of and away from _____. We would all put different things in this blank. Away from _____ (this world, my opinion, unthankfulness).

We have all seen a wedding and when the bride enters the sanctuary we see a beautiful woman — hair, makeup, and dress — all perfect. We have no idea what exactly she has gone through, but when she enters the room, we are not thinking of her past, only her future.

From what transpired over the next two weeks is still bearing fruit today months later. After coming home, I met with one of my dear friends to tell her about the retreat. One of the notes I had jotted down was to study, take a look at Rachel in the Word.

Rachel was only mentioned maybe once or twice, so I said to my friend, "I am not sure what the Lord is saying, but I need to look into that." A week or so after sharing with her, I was reading a book, and it began to talk about Rachel weeping for her children. Something went "pong" in my spirit, and I thought, "I need to find out more about Rachel." [Tish then went on to describe a personal event in her family that allowed her to enter into the weeping of Rachel for her own children through intercession. Rachel is a type of the bridal heart. [Since Tish's story was intimate in nature, I gave this summary. She ended her testimony by saying]: I am so thankful to all of you for your encouragement and love.

*— Tish*

*Testimony #4*

Elaine and I first met due to a series of conversations with mutual friends over the span of years, which ultimately inspired me to contact her. Hearing from both of our mutual friends that she and I were very similar in the things of the Spirit (both seeing into the third heaven, the Lord, angels, demons, having dreams and visions, releasing the prophetic word of the Lord, other gifts, and as well as living a prophetic lifestyle of intimacy with Holy Spirit), I wanted to know her. I was excited at the possibilities of meeting someone like me. I had never met anyone with those same extraordinary and unique Holy Spirit gifts that I could freely share what I saw, heard, and knew, etc., in my encounters and life with the Lord. She was truly the first who understood me and had wisdom for me, and many other gifts. I am richly blessed in her generosity and love for me and the way she shares her life with the Lord with me.

When I first wrote to Elaine, Holy Spirit gave me a prophetic word concerning her life and the new oil and fragrance He was bringing into her life for the new things He was doing. I wrote all that He said and told her about the new fragrance He was giving her and the fire of the Lord that He was going to ignite in her. I wrote many things that I do not remember now, but she understood and was blessed by all that the Lord was saying. She wrote and confirmed every word to me. I had no idea that Elaine was actually receiving new oils for the emerging bride and that this word had a tangible manifestation of what Holy Spirit was doing in the realms of the Spirit within and then through her, as well.

Elaine received the word and immediately responded with open arms for me, and, thus, our friendship began across the miles. She responded in love and has since repeatedly offered me great encouragement in kindness and love. She is a mother to me, a general to the generals in the Body of Christ, and a mother to the Bride as well as the Bride of our Lord Yeshua, Jesus Messiah. We have continued as friends and speak into one another's lives the word Holy Spirit releases, praying together, seeking His counsel and wisdom, for all our concerns in life. We've also had many encounters with the Lord together while in conversation and prayer on the phone, as we are in two different cities and time zones. I love it when we pray together. Something wonderful always happens.

Very soon after our initial meeting via e-mail, in a conversation on the phone, Elaine shared with me that she would be hosting an Emerging Bride Conference over a weekend in Upstate New York in July. As she shared more about what Holy Spirit had given her for the gathering I felt great excitement and desire to attend. During prayer, in another conversation with our mutual friend Mary, I had a vision where I saw myself standing outside a farmhouse looking into a window where I saw a beautiful white cloud which had filled the room, and knew the glory of the Lord was what that cloud represented. I told Mary what I was seeing, and I knew that farmhouse was the place where Elaine would host the bridal gathering. Once I saw the presence of the Lord (in that cloud), I asked Holy Spirit to take me to the farmhouse and meet me there in that cloud. That is exactly what the Lord did in that same year, at the Emerging Bridal Gathering Elaine held in the farmhouse. The Lord was there in beautiful glory and power. I fell in love even more with Him during my time there.

That summer Mary and I visited the farm and stayed for two weeks. Our time there was filled with peace, joy, and the amazing and awe of the presence of the Lord. Many wonderful things happened, but that would be far too much to write here. I'll just share some high points.

In our time together, days before the rest of the women arrived for the bridal gathering, Elaine, Mary, and I spent time in worship and resting, waiting on the Lord. Prior to our time together, we had each completed a twenty-one-day Daniel fast in preparation and were excited for all that Holy Spirit would do. We were not disappointed! A friend from North Carolina came and spent a couple of days with us, prophesying, teaching, and praying with us. We, in turn, did the same for him. It was rich and delightful blessing for all. As we worshipped together, the first evening of his time with us, the presence of the Lord came in such glory that we were unable to stand on our feet.

When he arrived at the farmhouse, he said he could feel the presence of the Lord and the glory of Yahweh before he stepped into the house.

Mary, Elaine, and I were already lying on the floor in the presence of the Lord as we continued in worship.

Within moments of our visitor's arrival, as our worship continued, I was fully surrounded and enveloped by the very cloud that I had seen in my vision, and in indescribable joy and ecstasy. I had never experienced more pleasure and joy in my life. *"At His right hand are pleasures forevermore,"* and I was fully in a bliss encounter with the Lord in a way that I had never known, imagined, or dreamed possible. I didn't know Holy Spirit would impact and overtake me in that way. No one could ever describe to me a bliss encounter with our Lord, and I apologize that I am unable to describe it well to you, dear reader. I will say, however, that I felt more pleasure than ever before or since in my life, and I have known all of the pleasures in life. Even though I thought that I might die because of His bliss, I shouted repeatedly, "If I die, I die! More, Lord! I want more of You! I must have more of You!" I was laughing hysterically and lost every bit of self-awareness, insecurity, and self-consciousness, and my body, spirit, and soul were fully in bliss. All that I cared about was the overwhelming encounter with beautiful Holy Spirit. Brilliant joy overtook me, and I lost track of everything ... everything, that is, except Him.

Elaine was in her own powerful encounter with Holy Spirit and shared how she was walking around in a rainbow. Wow! I was in what I call a whiteout because all that I could see was beautiful light, almost blinding, but I was able to look right into it. She was talking to the Lord, and I could hear her. As she described the rainbow she was seeing, I was in such brilliant joy and glory that I could not open my eyes. The light of God was blinding and yet I didn't care. I saw nothing but light. *"God is Light, and in Him there is no darkness at all."*

I have seen the Lord many times and on this occasion, I only saw His light and experienced His blissful love in a way that I had never known. This was not a sexual encounter, as some would believe. In this physical realm, we have no real grid for the things of the Spirit. This Holy encounter enveloped my whole being — body, soul, and spirit. I experienced more joy, love, freedom, peace, and overwhelming ecstasy than I can convey. When I asked the Lord later why He would overtake me in such ecstasy, He responded that this was His bliss. His bliss, He said, was reserved for those who give everything in life for Him. Then I understood the delight of the Lord. This is His delight in me. I have given everything and my life thus far to be His. I will give my all. That is my destiny.

Our worship lasted for a very long time that night. I was undone, to say the least, in the presence of the Lord and the brilliant joy that filled me. He continued to increase His presence within me during our bridal gathering. I found I was filled with even more delight and love for Him than before, which I didn't know was possible. I was changed in His presence during our gathering and came back home to the Midwest with an increase in His presence within and through me.

Even though these things may sound odd, far-fetched, or perhaps even ridiculous to some, I promise you that the realms of the Spirit of God (Yahweh) are not the same as the physical plane of this world. Holy Spirit manifested in some simple and not so simple ways during our time in our bridal gathering on the farm. He met us each one as we were able to receive Him.

At the end of our gathering on the farm, I had another experience I will share with you. I stood in the backyard, under the night sky, a blanket of stars overhead, and saw a company of angels stretched out before me. Holy Spirit gave me the understanding that they were there watching as

I made my salt covenant with the Lord, declaring and dedicating the rest of my life to Jehovah for His glory. The angels looked on with a sober countenance, all of them. They watched in silence and did not move, as I spent this sacred moment in time with the Lord under the *chuppah*, in the silence of my surroundings. The only sound was my voice, singing to the Lord, and the crickets in the summer grass and fields chirping along with their song.

As I entered the *chuppah* to give my life to the Lord as His Bride, I felt the eyes of the watchers upon me. I knew Holy Spirit allowed me to see only the angels of the Lord, but I felt the enemy there, as well. Fear had come to derail my covenant, but I refused to receive fear. This dedication had been ordained from long ago, by my holy Lord Yeshua, for His glory. I embarked on my journey from there with an even greater understanding of my life, and a greater sobering awareness that my life truly belongs to the King of Kings and Lord of Lords.

As I finished making my salt covenant with the Lord, singing my song to Him, vowing the rest of my life as His, the angels stood motionless. I turned to face them, and Holy Spirit gave me a flash in time, and I saw Stephen, the first martyr of the Church in the book of Acts. I watched as the angry crowd stoned him to death and saw Yeshua, Jesus, Messiah standing in Heaven, waiting to take Stephen home. I knew that Stephen felt no pain. He loved them and cried out for their forgiveness before his life was taken. He had great joy in seeing the Lord standing in Heaven ready to welcome Him home. I knew, from this encounter with the Lord and His angels, that the angels there with me at that moment would walk with me throughout my journey with the Lord all the days of my life, and that when my time came to depart this life, they would be with me, just like they were with Stephen. I knew that if I were martyred, I would feel no pain, and I would be taken to where the Lord stood waiting for me. In some ways, I saw my life stretched out before me and the messengers and the warriors that would be with me, doing the will of my Father in Heaven, so that I might finish well for His glory. In my experience under the *chuppah* with the Lord, Holy Spirit imparted His fire into my will. His all-consuming fire has been burning in me that I will do what the Lord does, say what He says, go where He goes, and live fully yielded in His love for my lifetime. His fire has continued working in me and my will since the Lord came to me in the *chuppah,* under a blanket of stars in that night sky in Upstate New York on the farm dedicated to the Lord and His work.

The Bridal Gathering brought us together from various places around the USA and Canada. We were a simple group of women of various ages that shared a desire to know the Lord more, be His faithful Bride, and share Him with all that would receive Him. Even though our experiences vary, I am confident that we were all encountered by our King of Glory. We were changed in His presence, as we worshipped and sang and rested in Him, waiting for His presence to overtake us in His all-consuming fiery love.

As Gloria anointed us with the perfumed oils Holy Spirit had given her, I was once again undone and had an experience with the Lord that is beyond words and not for everyone to hear. It remains a powerful and sacred time that we shared in the farmhouse and under the *chuppah*. I fell in love with the Lord even more during our time together and made friendships with some there that continue to grow and lead us together closer to living the life He has for each of us. We came into a partnership as His Bride in that precious gathering, and I pray that we go on to know the Lord more and love Him with all of our heart, might, mind, and strength, and also that we may love our neighbor as our self. I pray that we love the one in front of us, every single one of them. To God (Yahweh) be the glory for the great things He has surely done through Yeshua, Jesus, Messiah. May the Spirit and the bride say "Come! Come, King of Glory!"                    — *Linda Vaughan*

### *Testimony #5*

I was privileged to be a part of the Emerging Bride Gathering held in Ogdensburg, New York, on July 10, 2010. We were all called by God to be in this Bridal company and share in an encounter with the Lord. The instant comradeship and easy flow of the Spirit set the stage as the songs, ten anointing oils (poured on us by Gloria) and the time on the threshing floor got us prepared. What had God prepared for each of us? More than our hearts desire.

I had a pretty hat with a veil I bought for the occasion. One of the younger girls wore a wedding dress symbolically, and another veil as we worshipped. The marriage ceremony with the Lord was my desire. The wedding invitation and saying yes to the Lord and the intimate time under the *chuppah* (the marriage canopy) brought me a feeling of love, a love that was timeless, a love that was special, a love that brought me peace, a love I longed for and received. What more would any woman want? Nothing.

We received God's love, but more than this, we did it together. As we watched in awe and we danced together, we hated to part. It was called a five-star-general's meeting and a summit orchestrated by God. Thank you from the bottom of my heart.

*CGIT (Canadian Girl in Training)*
*Training for Reigning!*
*— Margriet Hintz*

## Sixteen Brides
### by Margriet Hintz

*Sixteen Brides came to this place,*
*Not knowing what they had to face,*
*Awakened brides, a new station,*
*Breaking ground at this location.*

*The Pennsylvania girls came from afar,*
*With Dorcas in her Hummer car.*
*Three girls flew in like a bird,*
*Bringing treasures from His Word.*

*The banquet was ready, everything complete.*
*Although it was hot, we got through the heat.*
*Angels welcomed us at the door,*
*And none of us wanted anything more.*

*We danced in the River and cried with joy.*
*It compared to the time the doctor said, "It's a boy!"*
*Gloria anointed us with ten different oils.*
*It felt like after a battle when we got the spoils.*

*Showers of blessings came to us all,*
*All because we had answered His call.*
*Quiet time in the* chuppah *at night was our delight.*
*As He spoke to each one, we loved Him with all our might.*
*Now we are parting, and it gives us inner pain,*
*But Yahweh gave us His power to reign.*
*This Bridal Company is now complete,*
*And the hope that we will once again meet.*

Here is the prophecy given for Upstate New York that Mary Ellen sent from the Elijah List:

*You will see the first light of this dawn. From the Canadian border will flow healing, power gifts, and mighty awakeners!*
*Look to the land of the north, for there My glory will stream forth. [This is what I saw too.] Many of my greatest gifts will come to you, and the days of Finney will be repeated times ten. The Bride will rise and shine like the sun, fair as the moon. You will come up out of your wilderness leaning on your Beloved. The dawning light is about to burst forth from the womb of the morning as the new day appears.*

*Threads of gold*

*I lie awake upon my bed,*
*Thoughts of You beholding me near.*
*Why can I not be comfortable here?*
*It's You my heart wants,*
*You my heart wishes.*
*All these tattered threads have made incomplete finishes.*
*None could have told me, nor whispered fine truths.*
*All winds have wrought me through Your divine sleuth,*
*Scattered and torn,*
*Broken but bruised …*
*How can any of this even be used?*

*Sparkles appear, as if on heavenly air,*
*Faint,*
*Almost invisible,*
*Yet suns glinting on them fair.*
*Swirls of light-orchestrating rhythms,*
*Movements and sounds,*
*Some being hidden,*

*Giggles of laughter,*
*Childlike squeals of joy,*
*Clasped hands in wonder,*
*Eyes watch the Divine ploy.*
*You reverse evil intentions,*
*What brought a life deep heartache and pain.*
*Suddenly, almost mysteriously,*
*Each loss transitions into gain.*
*What once was lamented, tattered and old*
*Spun wondrously,*
*Weaved marvelously*
*Into supernatural*
***Threads of gold***
— JOJO

For Elaine Perry
4.16.13
4 — His number for creation
16 — His number for LOVE (John 3:16 and 1 John 4:16)
13 — Divinity one hundredfold

## *For Glory and For Beauty* Presents:

Fragrances released to represent the Emerging Bride:

- *Eternal Flame* (Song of Songs 8:6)
- *Radiant* (Psalm 34:5)
- *Ravished Heart* (Song of Songs 4:9)
- *My Portion* (Psalm 16:5)
- *Spice Garden* (Song of Songs 4:16)
- *Under His Wings* (Psalm 91)
- *Two Camps* (Song of Songs 6:13)
- *Travail* (Isaiah 66:7)
- *Sheltered* (Psalm 61:3)
- *Honey in the Rock* (Psalm 81)
- *For Glory and for Beauty* (Exodus 28:2)
- *Oil of Forgiveness*
- *Hidden Treasures* (Isaiah 45:3)
- *Strength of the Vine* (John 15)
- *To Contend* (Isaiah 49:25)
- *Possessing the Gates* (Isaiah 45:1)
- *King's Garments* (Psalm 45:3)
- *Crown and Scepter* (Esther)
- *My Ishi* (Hosea 2:16)
- *Alabaster Jar* (Luke 7:37-38 and 46)

Regular price, $15.00 for 1/3 oz.

Special discount for book purchase 20% or $3.00.

USE SPECIAL OFFER CODE 5774

*Other oils available upon request.*

GLORIAREID26@AOL.COM

703-347-2446

# *Endnotes*

1. Roundtree, Anna, *The Priestly Bride* (Lake Mary, Florida, Charisma House Publisher: 2001)
2. Lyrics by J.W. Van Deventer, music by W.S. Weeden
3. Lyrics and music by Anna B. Warner, 1860
4. Weins, Gary, *Longing*, no date
5. Candler, Dana, *Deep unto Deep* (Kansas City, Missouri, Forerunner Publishing: 2001)
6. <http://www.myjewishlearning.com/life/Life_Events/Conversion/Conversion_Process/Mikveh.shtml>
7. Milligan, Ira, *Understanding the Dreams You Dream* (Shippensburg, Pennsylvania, Destiny Image Publishers: 1997)
8. Ryken, Leland; Wilhoit, James C.; and Longman, Tremper III, editors, *The Dictionary of Biblical Imagery* (Downers Grove, Illinois, InterVarsity Press: 1998)
9. Lyrics by Civilla D. Martin, music by Charles H. Gabriel.
10. <http://en.wikipedia.org/wiki/Ketubah>
11. Oates, Kathy, *Healing of the Heart,* unknown
12. Sanford, John and Paula, *Healing the Wounded Spirit* (Tulsa, Oklahoma, Victory House Publisher: 1984)
13. Ibid
14. Ibid
15. Ibid
16. Ibid
17. Malone, Henry, *Shame* (Lewisville, Texas, Vision Life Publications: 2006)
18. Cox, Paul, Aslan's Place, The Elijah List
19. Malone
20. Burk, Arthur; Gunter, Sylvia, *Blessing Your Spirit* (Birmingham, Alabama, The Father's Business: 2005)
21. <http://aslansplace.com/>